W9-CAY-671

THE WORLD OF ZEN

THE WORLD OF ZEN

STEPHEN HODGE

A GODSFIELD BOOK

Library of Congress Cataloging-in-Publication Data Available

10 9 8 7 6 5 4 3 2 1

Published in 2000 by
Sterling Publishing Company, Inc.
387 Park Avenue South, New York, N.Y. 10016

© 2000 Godsfield Press
Text © Stephen Hodge

Illustrations **Jane Hadfield**
Models **Mark Jamieson**
Picture research **Liz Eddison**
Photography **Ian Parsons, Guy Ryecart**

Stephen Hodge asserts the moral right
to be identified as the author of this work.

Every effort has been made to ensure that all the information in this book is accurate.
However, due to differing conditions, tools, and individual skills,
the publisher cannot be responsible for any injuries, losses, and other damages
which may result from the use of information in this book.

Designed for Godsfield Press by
The Bridgewater Book Company

The publishers wish to thank the following for the use of pictures:
Sarah Howerd, pp.2, 44; **Tony Stone**, pp.5, 8, 9, 13, 18, 19, 20, 23, 30, 32, 34, 41, 42, 48,
50, 61, 62, 70, 72, 73, 84, 85, 88, 90, 92, 93, 94, 102, 103, 106, 112, 113, 120, 126, 138;
Trip, pp.5, 10, 12, 26, 74 (H Rogers), 6 (D Harding), 36 (N Kealey, 37 (J Gilbert), 47 (T Bognar),
49 (B Vikander), 109 (A Tovy), 115, 118, 119, 124, 125, 127, 128, 129, 130, 147, 154;
Corbis, pp.14, 21, 22, 60, 64, 76, 123, 136, 137, 139, 140, 141, 149, 152, 153, 155, 157;
AKG, pp.28, 65, 89, 136; **Image Bank**, pp.34, 40, 51, 55, 66, 71, 98, 114, 142, 148;
Images, pp.54, 82; **Liz Eddison**, pp.132, 133; **et archive**, 134; **Werner Forman**, 146, 151

Printed and bound in China

ISBN 0–8069–2787–9

C O N T E N T S

INTRODUCTION

Over the course of its short history in the West, Zen has come to mean many things to different people. For some, it represents the core of the Buddhist path, free from all the cultural and intellectual trappings that can easily block and sidetrack people in their quest for spiritual growth. For others, it is a fashionable aesthetic experience with its emphasis on natural harmony and beauty, or else a secret weapon to be used in their martial arts training. In a way, Zen is all of these things and none of them, for the true Zen experience is not to be limited by individual perceptions that are based on incomplete judgements arising from an untrained ego-mind.

In this small book, I have tried to highlight a number of key areas where Zen has left its mark—obviously in the strictly religious aspect of meditation but also in its wider implications. The reader will not find much about Zen and motorbike maintenance here, but still I hope that everybody will find something of interest to them.

Although Zen originated in China, its influence there has been somewhat muted for complex historical reasons. So when we think of Zen, it is usually Zen culture in its Japanese guise that most readily comes to mind, for it was in Japan that it found its most enduring home.

It is supremely ironic that a form of Buddhism that devalued the use of words, through its emphasis on direct experience, should have given rise to so much literature. Perhaps it is the very mystery of Zen that prompts people to try and explain it so that they can neatly pigeonhole it in their minds. Some background reading is vital, in order to equip the reader with the necessary knowledge of the basic tenets of Buddhism upon which Zen relies, but soon books should be laid aside in favor of the meditation cushion.

This book will possibly provide the beginner with most of the basic facts they will need to make sense of Zen when they encounter it in the flesh, but obviously I have not been able to cover every single aspect that could have been included. In that respect, it is a personal selection based on my own early encounter with Zen practice in the United Kingdom, many years ago when I was in my early teens, and also on what I observed during a decade of life in Japan. Though I have undoubtedly had to unlearn much of what I thought I understood all those years ago, and though I now follow a different form of Buddhism, I feel that I have retained some things of value from that time. Foremost among these is an appreciation of the transience of life and the necessity to apply oneself to meditation practice while there is still the opportunity.

Humor should always be part of the Buddhist life, as these novice monks at the Bakong Temple in Cambodia demonstrate.

These days, there are many Zen instructors living in the West, some of whom have followed an authentic course of training, but there are also some who have not. Even in Japan nowadays, it is common for trainee Zen "teachers" to take shortcuts that would have been anathema a hundred years or so ago. It is characteristic of the Japanese to esteem an almost fanatical devotion to the "form" of things. If you follow the form correctly, then understanding will unfold naturally, or so they believe. Unfortunately, the form is often a lifeless shell from which the living essence has long since faded. So I believe it is dangerous for beginners to become too obsessed with the formalities of Zen practice—this leads to precisely the rigidity and lack of spontaneity that is the hallmark of incorrect Zen attainment. Thus I have noticed that many Western Zen trainees are over-serious in their practice and lack the most important mark of a Zen practitioner—a sense of humor. If you find a Zen group whose members do not laugh, then leave as soon as you can. Beware also the dictatorial or authoritarian teacher who is arrogant and cold, and lacks compassion and understanding of human nature.

I voice these concerns since they are real enough and have given rise to a controversial reappraisal of Buddhism in Japan known as Critical Buddhism through the efforts of Zen scholars like Noriaki Hakamaya and Shiro Matsumoto. Their main target of criticism is the uncritical, wishy-washy approach of many Buddhists in Japan to the humane ideals of Buddhism and their application in society. They note that, in Japan, some of the basic Zen concepts have been conveniently distorted and can no longer even be considered Buddhist at all. This is not the place to detail all of their arguments, but I feel that their call for a greater degree of social involvement, through the development of a sense of responsibility for the welfare of others, is vital—i.e. a keener development of loving kindness and compassion that is often lacking in some people's interpretation of Zen Buddhism.

I have tried in this book, therefore, to balance the cultivation of Zen with its practical application in the world at large. This is vital, since we now live on a rather small and overcrowded planet where Zen, at its best, can contribute something of real value.

Zen Buddhism should involve a deep understanding of loving kindness and compassion.

INDIAN ORIGINS

Such were the dramatic words of Ummon, one of the most revered Zen masters of China. Other Zen masters thundered that statues of the Buddha should be chopped up and burned, together with scrolls of the scriptures.

But this apparent iconoclasm merely conceals the essential dependence of Zen upon the Buddha, his Enlightenment and the teachings that arose from this experience. For it is also true to say that, without the Buddha, there would be no Zen; it is as much a product of the Buddha's teachings as any of the many other Buddhist schools that flourished over centuries in India and beyond. This means that, to understand Zen fully, we must first look at the life of the Buddha himself, what he taught, and then how his teachings were developed over hundreds of years in India before the unique approach of Zen was transmitted to China early in the sixth century.

Buddhism originated in India and its teachings were developed over several centuries before spreading to other countries in the region.

11

THE LIFE OF THE BUDDHA

Guatama received the title "Buddha" ("the Enlightened One") after attaining Enlightenment through meditation. (Early representation of Buddha in the Archaeological Museum, Sarnath, India)

Gautama, who was destined to become the Buddha, the Enlightened One, was probably born during the fifth century BCE at Lumbini in present-day Nepal. Born as the son and heir of a local ruler, Gautama was brought up in the midst of luxury and comfort. A sage had predicted that Gautama would become either a great emperor or sage when he reached adulthood, so his father decided to do all in his power to prevent his son from becoming a wandering sage. It seemed as though his father might succeed in his plans, for the Buddha later related that he spent his entire youth and early adulthood within the confines of the palace grounds. He married and had a son of his own.

Yet some nagging curiosity must have been gnawing away inside the depths of his being, and he began to wonder about the lives of ordinary people outside the walls of the palace. He ordered his charioteer to take him out secretly so that he could see things for himself.

What Gautama beheld had a profound impact on his hitherto sheltered life. He was to make four consecutive excursions, each of which revealed to him the harsh realities of human existence. On the first trip, he saw an old person, and subsequently a sick and diseased man, then a corpse being carried to be cremated. In confusion, he asked his charioteer about these sights and was told simply that such is the norm of everyday existence for every living creature. In despair and horror, he made one final trip out. On this occasion, he saw a wandering holy man striding serenely in the midst of the crowds.

Inspired by the sight of that wanderer, Gautama made up his mind to leave the palace rather than face the decay and death that he now realized awaited him. Leaving the palace late at night, he abandoned all of his finery and shaved off his hair.

He joined the ranks of the many spiritual seekers who flourished in India at that time determined to find a way out of the apparently inevitable misery of human existence. He visited many of the most noted teachers of his time, staying with them for a while to learn what he could from them. However, none of them seemed to have truly found the answer that he was seeking.

So he wandered by himself or in the company of a few companions, at times torturing his body with the severe ascetic practices that were common then. Yet still he was unable to reach the serenity and bliss that he sought.

The Enlightenment

Finally, six years after he had left his father's palace, Gautama found himself on the banks of the River Nairanjana, a small tributary of the Ganges. After refreshing himself with a light meal, he sat down under a fig tree and vowed to remain there until he had achieved the enlightenment that would answer of all his questions and bring an end to his frustrated longing for peace. Settling down in the evening, Gautama entered into a profound state of meditation and encountered a series of disturbing visions conjured up by Mara, the Tempter, in an attempt to prevent him from attaining his goal. But, overcoming these, he finally attained total enlightenment just as dawn broke the next morning. Henceforth, he was to be known by the title the Buddha (the Enlightened One). At that time he was thirty-two. He spent the rest of his life teaching others about the insights he had acquired into existence and the way in which all beings could eventually be freed from frustration and misery by achieving enlightenment for themselves.

Having attained total enlightenment at the age of thirty-two, the Buddha spent the rest of his life teaching his insights to others.

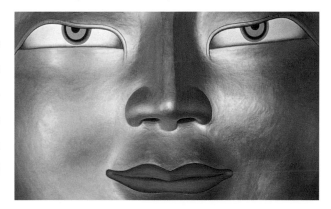

A Life of Teaching

Over the course of the following decades, until his death in his early eighties, the Buddha gave many different teachings, each suited to the ability and interests of his audience. He taught people from all walks of life and different levels of intelligence. Among his disciples were uneducated peasants, rich merchants, brahmin priests, kings and queens, and even a mass murderer. Though the content and style of his teachings varied, there were a number of core ideas that have been preserved to the present day by all Buddhists wherever they are in the world. An important thing to note at the outset about the Buddha's teachings is that everything he taught was based on what he had experienced personally. He did not claim to be a god or to have received any special revelations, but rather he always said that what he had achieved could also eventually be experienced by others. Another keynote of the Buddha's teachings was his insistence that people find out the truth of his teachings for themselves rather than blindly accepting his words out of reverence for him. He would say, "Try what I teach and see if it works for you!"

The Buddha devoted his life to teaching people from all walks of life and all levels of society.

The Three Characteristics of Life

A good point of entry into the Buddha's teachings would be three interconnected characteristics concerning everyday life: suffering, impermanence, and the absence of an ego-self. The idea that human existence is pervaded by suffering, misery, and frustration may seem far-fetched to many people living in the West, surrounded by comforts that their ancestors could not have imagined, even in their wildest dreams. Yet a quick look at the news on television or in the daily newspapers will soon show that we are indeed awash in a sea of misery worldwide—we are just a lucky and privileged few. At present, more than eighty percent of people in the world live in acute poverty in substandard housing, fifty percent suffer from malnutrition, while seventy percent are illiterate and have received virtually no education whatsoever. It is very possible that these statistics will worsen in the coming decades rather than improve, while a small minority seize the wealth of the planet for their own selfish ends. Yet even we who think ourselves immune from such misery and suffering will often be confronted, sometimes unexpectedly, with the pain that characterizes human existence. Though many of us have the good fortune to be free from the immediate misery of poverty, starvation, and war, careful reflection reveals that we still experience emotional unhappiness, a sense of emptiness in our lives, boredom, loneliness, and insecurity.

The Roots of Unhappiness

This simple yet profound observation by the Buddha led him to wonder why people tend to experience more unhappiness than happiness in their lives. Part of the answer is also quite simple: it is because all things are impermanent and ever-changing. This characteristic of existence is so obvious, when we think about it, and yet most people carry on with their lives as though everything lasts forever. Perhaps we notice the gradual process of aging, but still we continue as if we ourselves will never die. According to the Buddha, much of the misery and frustration that we experience arises through a mistaken belief in permanence. While we are happy, we think that our happiness can last forever, so when we lose whatever we have grown attached to, we then experience the pain of loss. In fact, were we to examine our lives carefully, we would not be surprised that things change. There are the gross physical changes of gradually growing old, then there are the almost moment-to-moment changes we can observe in our mental and emotional states. In the course of a single day, or even an hour, a myriad thoughts run through our heads, and our emotions may swing back and forth wildly.

The Illusion of an Ego-Self

The third and final characteristic of human existence is the non-existence or absence of an unchanging, independent ego-self, or what some call the soul. Through meditation techniques specifically designed for the purpose, we can see that there is no element, whether physical or mental, which can be identified as this ego-self. The Buddha did not deny that people have a sense of continued identity lying at the core of their being, but he believed that this ego-self is an illusory product of various conditions that have temporarily come together, and that interact for as long as we have a physical body. At the same time, we are often faced with a disturbing intuition that things are not as we would like. The ego-self seems to emerge as a defense mechanism to cope with the lack of control we have over our lives. Though the Buddha had to describe the three characteristics of life in a linear form, they are interwoven and are merely aspects of the same phenomenon. Change is a given fact of existence, so we try to hold onto things that are dear to us, and we experience pain when we lose them, and then we entrench ourselves further behind the protection of our ego-minds in a vain attempt to ward off that discomfort. This leads to greater attachment and greater possibilities of more suffering and frustration.

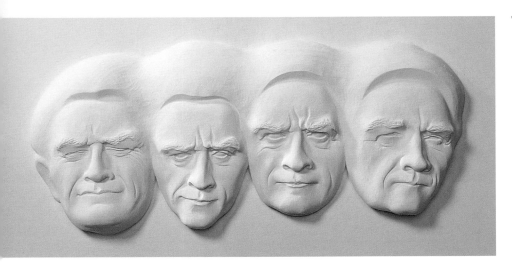

Our belief in an unchanging ego-self is an illusion that we generate to help us cope with change and uncertainty.

The Strategies of the Ego-Self

Looking at this process, the Buddha came to the conclusion that people have failed to understand the dynamics at work in their lives, and consequently they adopt strategies that can result only in failure. Indeed, he said that it was this very process that caused people to remain entrapped in a vicious circle of desperate measures and unwanted results.

It is usual for people to try to protect themselves from upsetting experiences. Buddhism teaches that there are three main methods that the ego-mind adopts in such cases. We may meet an apparently threatening or uncomfortable situation with aversion, the desire to shut it out, or destroy it; this is a way of distancing ourselves from it. Or we may attempt to control a situation through attachment; we try to engulf and overcome it by making it subordinate to our wishes and desires. The third alternative available to most people is simply to ignore the situation—to pretend it is not happening in the vain hope that it will disappear of its own accord. From these three basic strategies, which are viewed as pernicious and negative emotions in Buddhism, a whole host of subsidiary emotions are generated, such as jealousy, greed, and spite.

The Workings of Karma

These negative emotions provide the motivational power for our actions and are always preceded by a particular intention, which may be present below our threshold of awareness.

Naturally, some of our actions are set in motion by positive emotions, but this is generally not the case. The Buddha taught that, because our actions are charged with a sort of emotional energy, their effects go beyond the immediate results of which we are aware. Any action has an effect that goes beyond ourselves, but, at the same time, a feedback loop deposits some of that energy into our minds. If this is positive, then all is well and good, but this is not usually the case.

This deposit of energy in our minds will be released at some time in the future, when circumstances collude and trigger off further experiences that reflect the energy pattern of the original motivation. Buddhist scriptures describe this process in detail. Regardless of the specifics of an experience, negative motivations and actions lead to distressing and painful experiences, while positive ones have the opposite effect. The appropriate circumstances for enlightenment usually fail to arise during our present lifetime; we are all subject to rebirth, lifetime after lifetime, until the negative energy inside us has been exhausted. However, in ordinary life, we always create more and more negative energy, so the process never ends. This is the meaning of karma in Buddhism.

THE BUDDHA'S CURE

The Buddha is often compared to a great physician who examines a patient, diagnoses him or her, and then prescribes a course of treatment. Adopting traditional Indian therapeutic language, the Buddha taught a set of four observations about the human condition—the Four Noble Truths. First, he identifies the sickness: life is frustrating and filled with unhappiness for much of the time. Next, he specifies the cause of this suffering: attachment and clinging generated by the ego-mind. He then gives the good news: this condition is curable and peace is possible. Finally, he prescribes the treatment: the eightfold path, which details the areas of our lives where we can make changes, and how we should do this: through right understanding, right purpose, right speech, right conduct, right livelihood, right effort, right alertness, and right meditative concentration. These eight elements should be applied concurrently rather than as a consecutive sequence. Cultivated in the right manner, these eight elements gradually weaken, and eventually eliminate, negative emotions, and bring the cycle of continual rebirth to an end. When this happens, we may attain enlightenment and liberation from all suffering and negativity.

THE ROLE OF MEDITATION

Though morality and right living are important factors that enable us to lessen our individual burden of negative karmic energy, and thereby ease some of the discomfort we experience as human beings, most schools of Buddhism agree that meditation is essential to bring the whole process to an end. As Buddhism developed over the centuries, many different techniques for meditation were developed, but they all arise from two basic types of practice which are also central to the practice of Zen. The purpose of one is to develop calm and tranquillity, while the other leads to mindfulness and insight. Our normal everyday minds are filled with an uncontrolled torrent of thoughts and emotions, many of which are of very short duration. These often act as a kind of smokescreen, preventing us from focusing our minds on anything that might serve to undermine the carefully crafted illusion that all is well. Sudden outbursts of negative emotion usually take us by surprise; they also depend upon this stream of undisciplined mental activity. This makes the likelihood of continued negative actions and thoughts very probable. By concentrating our minds upon a single positive and wholesome object such as an image of the Buddha, a sacred sound, or, even more simply, upon the flow of our breathing, we can gradually learn to focus our thought processes, bring the outbursts of negative emotion under control, and experience a degree of calm and tranquillity.

By focusing on the purity of a single object, such as a lotus flower, we can bring negative thoughts and emotions under control.

Insight Meditation

Once we have gained the ability to keep our attention focused upon a single object for a reasonable length of time, it is possible to begin the other form of meditation which develops insight and mindfulness. It is the Buddhist view that the root of our existential predicament lies in the fact that we do not perceive anything in the world as it truly is, but rather live in a delusional pseudo-reality created by us through the ego-mind. Though the previous calming form of meditation serves to smooth things over and reduce major eruptions of negative emotions and thoughts, it cannot eliminate them completely. To do this, we must train ourselves to see things as they actually are, in order to develop the spiritual insight that reveals the true nature of the world. Again, many different techniques were taught for this purpose by the Buddha himself and developed by his later followers. However, all basically have the same aim: to cut through the fog of our pseudo-reality by applying the scalpel of insight, grounded in a firm grasp of the core Buddhist teachings mentioned above concerning the three characteristics of life: suffering, impermanence, and the absence of an ego-self. The task is not so much to think about impermanence, and so forth, but to see directly that these are all-pervasive facts of existence that we have chosen to ignore. We begin to see that our usual strategies, based on the demands of our ego-minds, are completely unreliable and ultimately lead only to disappointment. Instead of acting as though everything has some kind of permanence, we abandon ourselves to the stream of change. Instead of seeking to avoid suffering, we understand its causes and the way in which we bring it upon ourselves. Instead of holding tightly to the belief in a self-sufficient ego-mind, we begin to see that all things are interdependent, each event arising through a host of mutually interacting conditions.

THE DEVELOPMENT OF THE TEACHINGS

Such are the key doctrines of Buddhism, transmitted down the ages since the Buddha's lifetime. In the first few centuries after the passing of the Buddha, his followers seem to have applied themselves zealously to the path in their search for peace and liberation from the cycle of life. But, as time went by, and the Buddhist community grew in size and settled down in monastic settlements, various groups of monks with their own agendas emerged. There were some who continued to devote their energies to meditation, as had generations of monks before them, quietly seeking their own salvation. Others pursued scholastic studies of the *sutras*, the scriptures that recorded the teachings of the Buddha. They extracted the various doctrinal teachings that were scattered throughout the *sutras* and arranged these into convenient lists. To these, they then added comments and explanatory material, thus producing the various *Abhidharma* collections. Rather than practicing meditation, or even studying the *sutras*, these scholar monks focused all of their attention on subtle doctrinal matters and debates with other scholars, both within the Buddhist fold and without. Besides these two groups of monks, there was a third group who criticized their colleagues for what they saw as a betrayal of the Buddha's message. Although these monks acknowledged that meditation and study were important, they said that such pursuits were rather limited, as they tended to become ends in themselves.

For some monks, scholarly debate about the Buddha's teachings became an end in itself.

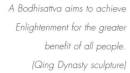

A Bodhisattva aims to achieve Enlightenment for the greater benefit of all people. (Qing Dynasty sculpture)

THE BODHISATTVA IDEAL

This third group of monks took the life and career of the Buddha himself as a model for a new spiritual ideal: the Bodhisattva. A Bodhisattva is a person who aims to achieve supreme Enlightenment, not so much for himself but in order to bring about the maximum benefit to other living beings. Whereas other types of monks were somewhat self-centered in their concerns, either for their own peace and liberation or for scholastic knowledge, this new movement tried to embrace all people, whether clerical or lay, male or female. They taught that the chief concerns of a Bodhisattva should involve the simultaneous cultivation of compassion and insight. Its adherents termed their approach the "Mahayana" (the Great Way), in contrast to the less ambitious one of the other monks which they called the "Hinayana" (the Lesser Way). Their approach may be summarized in a famous verse (*right*), which is chanted to this day by Zen practitioners, who are counted as Mahayana followers.

This form of Buddhism probably emerged as a distinct group around the early first century BCE, and flourished thereafter in India until the demise of Buddhism there in the face of the Muslim onslaught in the eleventh century CE. Its teachings also spread to many other Asian countries, such as Tibet, China, Korea, and Japan, where they continued through the centuries to the present day in various forms.

*HOWEVER INNUMERABLE SENTIENT BEINGS,
I VOW TO SAVE THEM ALL!
HOWEVER INEXHAUSTIBLE NEGATIVE EMOTIONS,
I VOW TO EXTINGUISH THEM ALL!
HOWEVER IMMEASURABLE THE TEACHINGS,
I VOW TO MASTER THEM ALL!
HOWEVER INCOMPARABLE
THE WAY OF THE BUDDHA,
I VOW TO ATTAIN IT!*

THE NEW SCRIPTURES

Though the followers of the Mahayana path retained much of earlier Buddhism, and, indeed, revitalized many of the neglected doctrines, they were also great innovators. In order to propagate their views, they created a large new body of scriptural literature dealing with the various aspects of their approach. This literature was attributed to the Buddha himself, though it is unlikely that he was the author. These texts are best seen as a way of presenting old teachings in a new way in order to attract converts. Some of them deal with the path and practices of the Bodhisattva and stress the need for compassion, selflessness, and high moral ideals. Others function as critiques of the scholasticism that had come to dominate the intellectual life of Buddhist monasteries, while others presented new models for understanding the workings of the human mind.

A number of these scriptures were highly prized by later Zen practitioners in China and elsewhere, so it will be useful at this point to look briefly at the themes of several of them. One such text is popularly known as the *Diamond Cutter Sutra*, which forms a part of a larger corpus of early Mahayana scriptures known as the *Perfection of Insight Sutras*. They all deal with the difficult concept of "emptiness" and how a Bodhisattva should cultivate it. The concept of "emptiness" can be found in the earliest Buddhist texts, but only comes to the forefront in Mahayana works. In its Mahayana presentation, it can be seen as a radical rephrasing of the Buddha's teachings concerning impermanence and the non-existence of a permanent and independent self. As a means of establishing the non-existence of an ego-self, the Buddha taught several systems for deconstructing the person into component elements. For example, he said the individual is composed of five psycho-physical components: matter, feeling, ideation, motivations, and consciousness. Through meditation, it can be established that none of these elements can be identified as the ego-self, as they are each impermanent. These five psycho-physical components can also be presented in greater detail, but the result is always the same: there is no self. The same analytical process, breaking down wholes into parts, was also applied to the world at large in order to overcome attachment. This process somewhat resembles the analysis of matter by

Just as a great body of water is composed of many tiny droplets, so, too, the self can be thought of in terms of its component elements.

chemists, which results in the periodic table of elements. The problem was that later scholar monks accepted that neither the individual nor the world had any permanent identity as gross phenomena, but they tended to believe that the constituent parts were real. The Mahayana view is that even these component elements are devoid of any true or substantial reality; at best, they are merely convenient labels that can be used for descriptive purposes. This total lack of abiding reality behind persons and objects on any level is what is meant by "emptiness." The relatively short *Diamond Cutter Sutra* presents this concept as it affects the Bodhisattva practice, and uses enigmatic paradoxical language to describe the world of the Bodhisattva. It also highlights the need for the special kind of insight known as *prajña* that a Bodhisattva needs in order to "realize" emptiness.

THE LANKAVATARA SUTRA

Another Mahayana scriptural text that was later influential in Zen is the *Lankavatara Sutra*. This is a much longer work, and covers a wide range of topics, mainly concerned with the nature of the mind and its relationship to reality and Enlightenment. Drawing on earlier trends in Mahayana, the *Lankavatara Sutra* teaches that everything in the world that we normally experience is delusional, resulting from false images projected outward by the dualistic operations of the everyday mind, in a manner similar to dreams. In other words, due to profound spiritual ignorance, a split occurs in the mind, and two poles are established: the self which perceives, and the objects perceived by it. However, this split is false and does not reflect the intrinsic state of the mind which the *Lankavatara Sutra* teaches is pure and inherently enlightened. This inherently enlightened mind is also known as Buddha nature, a concept that subsequently became of great importance in Zen Buddhism. In fact, not only are the minds of all beings inherently endowed with Buddha nature, but all things are also said to be endowed with Buddha nature, because they are projections of the mind. This view of Buddha nature has led to criticism from some quarters as it seems to contradict the key doctrine that all things are devoid of any underlying unchanging identity.

Although the everyday mind projects its own delusions onto the world, in its true state the mind is pure and enlightened.

THE VIMALAKIRTI SUTRA

Buddhist scriptures teach that insight and compassion will lead to a new spiritual awakening in the world.

Two other scriptures are held in high esteem by Zen practitioners: the *Vimalakirti Sutra* and the *Avatamsaka Sutra*. The *Vimalakirti Sutra* is a fairly short work which presents the teachings on emptiness in a dramatic manner. Vimalakirti is the name of a highly accomplished layman, who is actually a Bodhisattva, whose understanding of emptiness completely transcends that of the other members of the Buddha's entourage. This aspect of the text is important, because it shows that the goal of Buddhism is open to lay people who may surpass the specialist, "professional" Buddhists who are monks. The text takes the form of a series of dramatic encounters between Vimalakirti, who is feigning illness, and various people who come to visit him. Each of these people were famed as experts in their chosen area of Buddhism, but Vimalakirti shows them that their understanding is limited and leads to contradictions. In this sense, the *Vimalakirti Sutra* shows how a Bodhisattva is to use insight and compassion in the world as a means to liberation.

THE AVATAMSAKA SUTRA

The *Avatamsaka*, or *Flower Garland Sutra*, is the title given to a very large compilation of texts that were probably in circulation as independent scriptures. Many of these works show an understanding of reality similar to that taught in the *Lankavatara Sutra*. Among them, the latter part of the *Avatamsaka Sutra* concerns the journey to Enlightenment of a youth called Sudhana. Over the course of his journey, he encounters over fifty different people from all walks of life who teach him what they understand of the Buddhist path to Enlightenment. The appeal to the followers of Zen lies especially in the vision of vast universes populated by Buddhas and their followers. It is said that these descriptions served as a means for Zen practitioners to measure their own achievements.

Of necessity, the descriptions here of these four scriptures can only hint at their contents, but fortunately they are readily available in English translation. The reader is strongly urged to read them, possibly starting with the more accessible *Vimalakirti Sutra*. Although, as we shall see, proponents of some forms of Zen seem to be hostile to the study of scriptures, the influence of these *sutras* was extremely marked upon the development of Zen in China.

The Avatamsaka Sutra shows that we may encounter many teachers along the path to Enlightenment.

27

THE DEVELOPMENT
AND TEACHINGS OF **ZEN**

Following centuries of developments in its Indian homeland, Buddhism eventually reached China in the first century CE. At first, this exotic religion did not appeal to the mainstream of Chinese intelligentsia, but found wide support among ordinary people, especially in the various small kingdoms ruled by non-Han Chinese kings. Right from the start, the Chinese were fairly selective about what interested them, so, outside a small group of monks and scholars, much of the very technical and polemical Buddhist literature was poorly understood and little appreciated. It was not until the legendary monk Bodhidharma came to China in the fifth century and transmitted the distinctive teachings and practices of Zen that a truly distinctive national form of Buddhism developed in China. Though the overall content had its roots in Indian Buddhism, the Chinese added much that is derived from traditional Chinese philosophy, both from Confucianism and from Taoism.

A SPECIAL TRANSMISSION OUTSIDE THE SCRIPTURES, NOT DEPENDENT ON WORDS AND LETTERS— DIRECTLY POINTING TO THE REAL PERSON, IT ALLOWS YOU TO SEE INTO YOUR TRUE NATURE AND TO ATTAIN BUDDHAHOOD.

THE TRANSMISSION OF BUDDHISM TO CHINA

Though Buddhism had probably entered China by way of travelers along the Silk Road, tradition maintains that the Han emperor Ming Di (58–76 CE) had a dream of a golden deity flying through the sky. This was interpreted as a vision of the Buddha, so emissaries were despatched to India. They returned with teachings, and the first Buddhist text was translated into Chinese. Over the following few centuries, a number of Buddhist teachers made their way to China from Central Asia and India and devoted their energies to propagating Buddhist ideas. As China already had a long and sophisticated philosophical legacy, many Buddhist ideas were difficult for the Chinese to accept. As Taoism seemed to be conceptually the closest to Buddhism, many Buddhist ideas were expressed using Taoist terminology and concepts to make them intelligible to the Chinese. Indeed, many Chinese people at the time believed that Lao-tzu, the reputed founder of Taoism, had been reborn in India as the Buddha. However, this was very confusing, as Taoist beliefs are very different from Buddhist ones.

Buddhism reached China by way of travelers and teachers from India and other parts of Central Asia.

It was not until several hundred years had elapsed that Buddhism began to be transmitted to China accurately—a situation similar to that we now see in the West where Buddhism has only a short history. But, fortunately, several gifted monks from Central Asia, such as Kumarajiva, in collaboration with outstanding Chinese scholars, were able to present Buddhist teachings more accurately. During this period, from the first to the fifth centuries CE, Buddhism in India was undergoing important developments with the introduction of new innovative concepts and practices. It was during this period that the key Zen texts such as the *Lankavatara Sutra* and the *Diamond Cutter Sutra* were first translated.

Additionally, there was growing interest in India in the teachings about belief in Pure Lands connected with various Buddhas. A "Pure Land" is a kind of paradise created by the power of a Buddha as a safe haven for devotees to further their path to Enlightenment without the usual difficulties associated with life in our realm. The recitation of the name of the Buddha who created the relevant Pure Land was considered to be the guaranteed method for rebirth in such places. This was brought about by the power of the Buddha's compassion and desire to help beings.

BUDDHISM TAKES ROOT IN CHINA

By the sixth and seventh centuries CE, Buddhism had become well established in China, despite occasional setbacks that it suffered in the form of persecutions by emperors whose minds had been turned against Buddhism by jealous Taoist priests. All of the main Indian forms of Buddhism had been transmitted and absorbed in varying degrees. Indeed, a number of brave Chinese monks began making the arduous journey to India by land and sea. The Chinese did not blindly adopt everything imported from India but were quite selective. The mysticism of religious Taoism predisposed them to certain forms of Buddhism rather than others. Mahayana texts that spoke of splendid vistas of mystical experience and magical practices and which used the language of paradox seem to have been particularly attractive. Unlike neighboring Tibet, most Chinese never became interested in the study or use of logic, an area of Buddhist philosophy that was becoming very important in India at that time. Some would argue that this disinterest had a profoundly detrimental effect on the later course of Buddhism in China. But, despite this, many Chinese monks devoted enormous efforts to studying and annotating the Buddhist scriptures; perhaps it was the Chinese respect for the written word that led many monks to neglect meditation practice for mere book-learning.

As Buddhism became established in China, it developed a particular focus on the mysticism which was also important to Taoism.

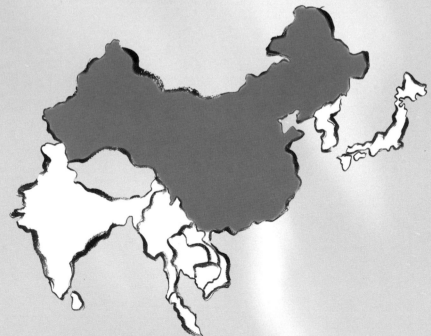

TRANSMISSION LINEAGES

We should not be too surprised at this development in China, for a similar situation had arisen in India several times during the long history of Buddhism there. It seems inevitable that some people will always be more inclined to the academic study of doctrines, while others will assert the primacy of religious practice and meditation. In India, the Pure Land devotees must have been among those who stressed the importance of action compared with theory. Similarly, there were no doubt many monks, nuns, and even lay followers who valued meditation more than anything else. We do not know the names of many of these people, since they did not leave books for posterity by which to remember them, so it is difficult to trace their history. Nevertheless, there are some allusions to such people in various sources. The most important of these are the various transmission lines preserved by various schools of Buddhism. In general terms, Buddhism lays great stress upon the idea of a lineage of teachers stretching right back to the Buddha Shakyamuni himself, for, in this way, the legitimacy of any particular line of teaching can be authenticated. Later, in China, followers of Zen claimed to have a special transmissional lineage of twenty-seven Indian patriarchs going back to the Buddha. The first patriarch was the wise old monk Kashyapa. One day, it is said, a great assembly of monks had gathered around the Buddha, eager to hear his teachings, full of expectations. But, on this occasion, the Buddha merely sat silently for some time and then raised up a small flower in his hand. Everybody present was perplexed and could not understand what was happening. All, that is, except for Kashyapa. He smiled, for he had experienced the great awakening that was later to be so highly treasured by Zen Buddhists. For, as the words of Bodhidharma state, Zen Buddhists say that their method is transmitted without words but by the power of mind alone.

BODHIDHARMA

Bodhidharma is the twenty-seventh patriarch in the Zen lineage. Historically reliable details about him are overshadowed by pious legends that grew up around events that occurred in his life. He is thought to have arrived at Guangzhou (or Canton) in southern China from India in 526 CE.

Later that year, the emperor Wu Di of the Liang dynasty invited him to the capital at Nanjing for an audience. By all accounts, the emperor was thoroughly mystified by the encounter, and was less than enthusiastic about Bodhidharma.

The emperor said that he had built many monasteries and temples and asked what merit he had earned thereby. To his astonishment, Bodhidharma replied, "None whatsoever!"

Then the emperor asked, "What is the meaning of the sacred Dharma?", to which Bodhidharma said, "Limitlessly open, nothing is sacred!"

The perplexed emperor posed one final question, "Then tell me who you are."

Bodhidharma's famous answer was, "I don't know." With this, the interview ended and Bodhidharma left for the north.

He crossed the Yangtze and ended up at the famous Shao-Lin Temple in Henan province. There he settled and spent the next nine years in deep meditation facing a wall, because, it is said, the time was not right for him to begin teaching.

Buddha taught that "Buddha nature" can be achieved by becoming impassive in the face of outside influences, like a wall.

BODHIDHARMA AND HUI-KE

One day, Bodhidharma was visited by a monk in his forties called Hui-ke. He begged Bodhidharma to become his teacher, but was ignored. It was winter, and Hui-ke stood outside the temple until the snow reached his knees. But still Bodhidharma seemed unconvinced of his sincerity. In desperation, Hui-ke took a sword and cut off his forearm, which he presented to Bodhidharma, and begged for teachings. The following dialogue is said to have ensued:

"My mind has no rest, Master, please help me pacify it!"

"Bring me your mind and I will pacify it for you."

"I have searched everywhere for it, but I cannot find it!"

"There! I have pacified your mind!"

Shortly after this Bodhidharma began teaching. Bodhidharma himself was not hostile to study, but taught that it should go hand-in-hand with practice. He especially esteemed the *Lankavatara Sutra*, which taught about the primordial purity of the mind and Buddha nature. Buddha nature, he said, is not manifest in ordinary beings, because it is enveloped by a dense covering of negative emotions such as greed, anger, and stupidity. When we understand this, we should devote ourselves to meditation and daily practice in order to remove these obstacles so that the primordial Buddha mind can shine forth in us. He is also reputed to have given the following core teaching to Hui-ke:

"Drop all discursive thoughts and all attachments. Rest your mind. Like a wall, do not be influenced by internal or external things; only then can you enter the path of the Buddha."

HUI-KE (487–593 CE)

Soon after, at the end of his stay in China, Bodhidharma chose his successors. Though each of those he tested had made impressive progress in their understanding of his teachings, only Hui-ke had fully grasped what Bodhidharma was trying to transmit. So it was to him that Bodhidharma passed the insignia of the patriarchs: the robe and begging bowl of the Buddha, the direct transmission by mind transcending words, and a copy of the *Lankavatara Sutra*. Thus, Hui-ke became the first Zen patriarch in China. The details concerning Hui-ke's later life are sparse. It is thought that he soon left Shao-Lin to live as a wanderer, while continuing to study the

profound *Lankavatara Sutra* and to cultivate meditation. Apparently his lifestyle was somewhat unorthodox, and he had to flee to the south of China to escape the ire of the authorities. Indeed, some sources say that he was eventually condemned to death and executed on charges of heresy brought against him by jealous orthodox monks. However, some time during his travels, Hui-ke encountered Seng-can, who was to become the third patriarch.

SENG-CAN (?–606 CE)

As is the case with his predecessors, little is reliably known about Seng-can's life. Legend has it that he suffered from leprosy. When he went to visit Hui-ke, their dialogue went as follows:

"My body is possessed by a mortal disease. Please, Master, wipe away my sins!"

"Bring me your sins and I'll wipe them away for you."

"I've looked for my sins, but I can't find them!"

"In that case, I have thoroughly wiped away your sins. Live now in accordance with the Three Jewels."

This incident is reported to be the moment when Hui-ke made the mind transmission to Seng-can, later confirming him as the third Chinese patriarch of Zen.

Many Buddhist monks were persecuted and killed by the Chinese authorities.

About 574 CE, there was violent persecution of Buddhism. In order to escape the capture and execution that had befallen many other monks, Seng-can feigned mental illness and took refuge in the mountains for ten years. Some of the earliest Zen writings are attributed to Seng-can, such as the *Xin-xin-ming*—"Illuminating the Faith of the Mind." The celebrated opening line of this text is frequently quoted, "The venerable way is not difficult; it only abhors picking and choosing." It also expresses the basic ideas of Zen in poetic form, and shows the beginnings of the strong Taoist influence or, some might say, distortion that was to become characteristic of later Zen in China and Japan. In fact, the teachings that passed as Taoism at that time had little to do with the original message of Lao-tzu and Zhuang-zi, but rather reflect Confucian misconceptions about their teachings. Thus the reader should note that many of the ideas in Zen Buddhism about the so-called Tao are not actually Taoist but reflect another interpretation of Confucian teachings!

DAO-XIN (580–651 CE) AND HUANG-REN (601–674 CE)

Seng-can's successor was Dao-xin, the fourth patriarch in China, who received the transmission from him while still young. Seng-can told Dao-xin to go and take up residence at the monastery at Mount Lu and to instruct students in *zazen* (seated meditation) and the *Lankavatara Sutra*. Some time later, Dao-xin had a vision which directed him to move to a nearby mountain called Shuang-feng. His fame attracted many students to him, and it was this that probably prompted Dao-xin to establish the first purely Zen monastery, which was to be self-sufficient and independent. This monastery paved the way for the foundation of many similar Zen communities. Under Dao-xin, this period in Zen's development in China marks a gradual shift away from orthodox Mahayana Buddhist teachings and practice, as he tended to play down the importance of scriptural study, while emphasizing the practice of *zazen*. Among his students was Huang-ren who, through his deep understanding of primordial awakening, was eventually chosen as the fifth patriarch. Under his tutelage, Zen practice and study continued to flourish at Mount Shuang-feng, and then at Mount Huang-mei.

The patriarch Dao-xin established the first of many monasteries throughout China such as this one.

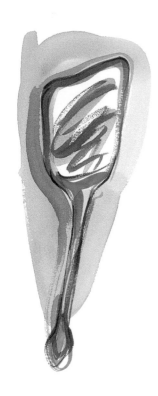

HUI-NENG (638–713 CE)

While Huang-ren was abbot at Huang-mei, he was visited one day by an illiterate young peasant called Hui-neng. He was so poor that he had had to support his widowed mother and himself by cutting and selling firewood. One day he had heard somebody chanting the *Diamond Cutter Sutra*, and, when he heard the line, "Let your mind flow freely without dwelling on anything," he had an experience of awakening (*kensho*). He resolved to find a teacher who would give him further instruction, and thus ended up at Huang-ren's monastery. Although he immediately made a profound impression on Huang-ren, it was thought improper for him to join the other monks formally, so he was given the menial job of pounding rice instead.

Some time later, Huang-ren decided that he wanted to select his successor, so he announced a contest in which everybody interested would write a short poem of realization expressing their understanding and put it up on a wall of the monastery. Another of Huang-ren's students, a learned monk called Shen-xiu, was expected to win, so nobody else bothered to compete. What Shen-xiu wrote was profound and reflected the type of Zen that had been practiced until the time of Huang-ren:

The body is like a bodhi tree and the mind a bright mirror;

carefully, we wipe them clean every day and let no dust alight.

Hui-neng then wrote a reply and secretly put it up alongside Shen-xiu's composition:

The body is not like a bodhi tree and there is no bright mirror;

since everything is empty from the start, where can the dust alight?

Through this poem, Hui-neng demonstrated that he had a full realization of emptiness, that, in reality, no distinction can be made between phenomena, whether they appear as objects or as the mind which perceives them. All the other monks were perplexed and wondered who had had the temerity to put up a challenge to the favorite, Shen-xiu. Yet Huang-ren himself knew there was only one person among all his students who had that level of accomplishment: Hui-neng.

THE BODY IS LIKE A BODHI TREE
AND THE MIND
A BRIGHT MIRROR;
CAREFULLY, WE WIPE THEM CLEAN
EVERY DAY AND
LET NO DUST ALIGHT.

THE BODY IS NOT LIKE
A BODHI TREE AND THERE
IS NO BRIGHT MIRROR;
SINCE EVERYTHING IS EMPTY
FROM THE START, WHERE
CAN THE DUST ALIGHT?

One night soon after, Huang-ren called Hui-neng to his room and bestowed upon him the symbols of the patriarchy: the robe and the bowl. Huang-ren realized that there would be great opposition to this illiterate outsider taking his place as the sixth patriarch, so he advised Hui-neng to leave immediately and hide out in safety in the south of China. Though, in fact, he was pursued by a group of angry monks, he is said to have overcome their hostility by a display of his deep understanding and powers as a teacher. After having spent some fifteen years in solitary meditation in the depths of the mountains, he went to the monastery of Fa-xin. There he heard two monks arguing about a flag fluttering in the wind. One monk insisted that it was the flag itself which was moving, while the other maintained that it was the wind which was moving. On hearing this, Hui-neng said to them,

It is neither the flag nor the wind that moves,

it is your mind that moves.

The abbot of this monastery realized that this was none other than Hui-neng, of whom he had heard. At this time Hui-neng had still not even been ordained as a monk, so the abbot arranged for him to take his vows and to teach his understanding of Zen at the Fa-xin monastery. Later, Hui-neng taught at his own monastery — the Bao-lin — which was near Canton in the south.

The robe and the begging bowl are passed down from one Zen master to the next as the symbols of the Buddha.

HUI-NENG'S ZEN AND THE *PLATFORM SUTRA*

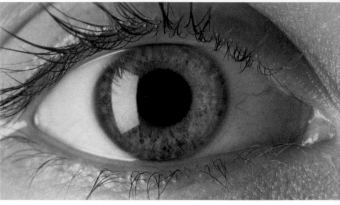

Although Zen practice and teachings prior to Hui-neng had taken on more and more local Chinese cultural coloring, it was with Hui-neng that Zen truly emerged out of its Indian guise. With him, Zen entered into its golden age in China. Possibly because he was originally an illiterate peasant, he completely rejected book-learning and any other form of scholarly erudition. At the same time, his style of teaching was practical, vigorous, and down-to-earth, with a good mixture of dry humor. One famous phrase is attributed to Hui-neng: "Seeing into one's own nature." This had been the implicit goal of Zen Buddhism in the past, but it became the essence of later teachings. According to Hui-neng, this seeing into one's nature or "Buddha mind" could be only an instantaneous event—not a gradual process.

The notion of "seeing into one's own nature" became a central teaching within Chinese Buddhism.

Although he was illiterate, Hui-neng's teachings, anecdotes, and lectures were recorded in a text known popularly as the *Platform Sutra*. Recent research on this text, using materials discovered early this century at Dun Huang, cast some doubts on the belief that the contents are all from Hui-neng himself, for the text is now known to have been expanded over the centuries with additional material. However, it is certain that the core of the teachings in the *Platform Sutra* do derive from Hui-neng's approach to Zen. One celebrated passage that sums up this approach is as follows:

WHEN THE SUDDEN DOCTRINE IS UNDERSTOOD,
THERE IS NO NEED TO DISCIPLINE YOURSELF
IN EXTERNAL THINGS.
IF YOU ALWAYS HAVE THE RIGHT VIEW
WITHIN YOUR MIND,
YOU WILL NEVER BE DELUDED.
THIS IS SEEING INTO YOUR OWN NATURE.

THE SPLIT INTO NORTHERN AND SOUTHERN SCHOOLS

Meanwhile, in the north, Huang-ren had died and the lineage there passed, as expected, to Shen-xiu. This resulted in the emergence of two rival systems of Zen: the Northern School and the Southern School. Although Hui-neng and Shen-xiu were on good terms with each other, the dispute about the validity of their respective methods eventually became quite bitter. The Northern School still maintained vestiges of the traditional Indian Mahayana approach to Enlightenment. Its followers advocated a gradual approach to Enlightenment through meditation, but accompanied by the study of scriptures such as the *Lankavatara Sutra*, the *Diamond Cutter Sutra*, and the *Avatamsaka*. The followers of the Northern School felt that these scriptures provided valuable pointers to the dynamics of the mind, and how it should be understood and trained. They also stressed the importance of conventional Buddhist morality and discipline, combined with good works for the benefit of ordinary people.

In contrast, the Southern School founded by Hui-neng defined itself as the "sudden" approach. Following Hui-neng's lead, his followers discarded virtually all scholarly study of scriptures, though they did esteem the *Diamond Cutter Sutra* to a degree. As Buddha mind is within everybody, it is not so much a question of achieving Enlightenment by a process of acquisition or gradual accumulation of merits and wisdom. Rather, one sudden and intuitive break-through is all that is needed to cut through the mass of deluding thoughts and emotions that veil the true mind. In this sense, the Southern School relied on direct and unmediated experience of reality, which would open the way for a practitioner's Enlightenment.

Although the Northern School survived for a while after Shen-xiu's death, it soon withered away into oblivion like so many earlier schools of Buddhism that were alien and inimical to the Chinese spirit, while Hui-neng's Southern School emerged as a unique Chinese form of Buddhism. This flourished and has continued to the present day through various lineages transmitted within China and in neighboring countries.

To achieve Enlightenment, we must break through the delusions that cloud our minds.

41

LIN-JI (?–866 CE)

Of the many subsidiary lineages that arose from Hui-neng's Southern School, two are of particular interest to us here: that which led to the Lin-ji school, and that which led to the Cao-dong school. After Hui-neng, all of his successors preoccupied themselves with trying to find new methods for triggering the necessary sudden awakening. One master, Ma-zu (709–788 CE), was famed as the inventor of "hard" Zen; he used many violent methods to awaken his students, which would have horrified Buddhist teachers in India: deafening shouts, punches, kicks, and beatings. To his lineage also belong other famous and venerated Zen masters such as Nan-sen, Huang-bo, and Zhao-zhou. But it is Huang-bo's successor, Lin-ji (?–866 CE), who founded one of the main lineages and styles of Zen that survives today.

Lin-ji continued the use of violent blows and shouts to awaken his students from their unenlightened state, but also he synthesized many of the methods utilized by his predecessors. One notable innovation that dates from the time of Lin-ji is the use of the *koan*. The term "koan" derives from the Chinese expression for a "public notice", which refers to legal cases that were used to establish precedents in law. In Zen, *koans* are mini-dialogues between famous Zen masters and their students, often reduced to their usually enigmatic punch lines. Many of these are extracted or derived from longer dialogues known as *mondo* or "questions and answers." They were used by Lin-ji and his successors as a means to push the student's mind in desperation beyond everyday rational thinking in an attempt to break through to the inherent Buddha mind.

Lin-ji's style may well have been symptomatic of the age, for, in 845 CE, mounting hostility from the authorities about the lax practices and antisocial behavior of orthodox Buddhist schools provoked a savage persecution that was to leave thousands of monks and nuns dead and huge numbers of temples demolished in an attempt to destroy Buddhism. In passing, it is strange to note that similar tactics are still being used by the Chinese authorities to suppress Buddhism in Tibet. Be that as it may, Zen was virtually the only school of Buddhism that was able to ride out the storm unharmed, as it did not especially depend upon monasteries or religious artifacts.

Cao-Dong School

In contrast to the robust style of Lin-ji and his use of *koans*, Dong-shan (807–869 CE) and his student Cao-shan (840–901 CE) founded the other main form of Zen Buddhism which survives today—the Cao-dong school. Living in the same era as Lin-ji, these two masters derived their descent from Hui-neng through the gentle Shi-tou (700–790 CE). In fact, Shi-tou had his monastic establishment in the same region as Ma-zu had his. The two seem to have conducted a kind of symbiotic operation, one acting as the "nice guy," and the other as the "bad guy." Each sent his students to the other for testing. Unlike the Lin-ji school, the Cao-dong school emphasizes silent meditation without much use of *koans*. Both of these founding masters of Cao-dong used gentle dialogues with their students in preference to the violence and harshness associated with Lin-ji and his successors.

Later Developments in China

The heyday of Zen in China was during the Tang and Song (960–1127 CE) dynasties. It was then that all the famous Zen masters were to emerge, and all the schools of Zen to develop.

However, as time went by, a decline inevitably set in. One symptom of this was the artificial intellectualism and culture that became popular in China during the Song period. This infected Zen practice and led to mere intellectual study and analysis of Zen teachings. Having lost its original vitality, Zen, like much of Chinese culture, was dealt a virtual death-blow with the invasion of the Mongols, who governed the country from 1279 CE for almost one hundred years. Although Buddhism survived this invasion and continued to flourish under the succeeding Ming and Qing dynasties, China's Mongolian rulers often had a strong faith in the Tibetan form of Buddhism, with its emphasis on rituals and Tantric practices. Zen itself survived only by merging with the Pure Land School, whose doctrines were once so inimical to Zen, and producing a syncretic form of Buddhism that is still practiced today. It is heartening to note there has been a recent revival of interest in all forms of Buddhism in China.

Zen has continued to flourish in
Vietnam, where it is known as
Thien, *since the sixth century* CE.

ZEN OUTSIDE CHINA

Though Zen went into gradual decline in China, it fared somewhat better in neighboring countries. Buddhism had entered Korea during the fourth century CE and produced many great monks, both scholars and practitioners. These monks frequently spent long periods of time studying in China, and a few even went farther afield—as far as India.

Zen reached Korea around the middle of the seventh century, and is known there as *Son*—the Korean pronunciation of the Chinese character for Zen. Just as in China, the predominant form of Son was derived from the Lin-ji lineage, although Cao-dong was also transmitted. Although not himself a direct participant in the Chinese Zen lineages, the greatest figure in Son history is probably Chinul (1158–1210 CE). Aware of the tensions that existed between Son and the other more orthodox schools, Chinul created a magnificent synthesis of their various views—which was to be predominant throughout the subsequent history of Buddhism in Korea. Without going into great detail here, what Chinul did was to find a way of combining the sudden and the gradual approaches. He taught that the initial breakthrough to an experience of the inherent Buddha-mind could be achieved suddenly, but then a gradual process of meditation and study was needed to deepen and strengthen the initial awakening. Through the untiring efforts of successive generations of Korean masters, Son has survived well into the present day, despite periodic persecutions in earlier centuries.

Zen was also introduced into Vietnam at the very early date of 580 CE, during the lifetime of the third Patriarch Seng-can, by the Indian monk Vinataruci, who had practiced Zen in China. Over the following centuries, many Vietnamese went to China to study Zen—or *Thien*, as it is known in Vietnamese—and some of them set up what were to become five separate lineages of Zen in Vietnam. Just as in Korea, there was an important syncretic school (founded by Thao-dong) which combined Thien with Pure Land doctrines. Unlike Buddhism in other countries, Thien, with its Pure Land component, has been the sole form of Buddhism practiced in Vietnam. The great modern master Thich Nhat Hanh is a truly impressive ambassador for the humane style of Vietnamese Thien.

Zen was introduced to Vietnam in 580 CE by an Indian monk.

But, of all the neighboring countries that received Zen teachings, the best known is Japan. Zen was transmitted to Japan during the peak of Zen development and vitality in China, and then remained in isolation, so Japanese Zen has in many respects preserved a more authentic form of Zen than that now practiced in China. The two main Chinese Zen lineages, Lin-ji and Cao-dong—or *Rinzai* and *Soto* as they are known in Japan—were taken across the sea to Japan, where they have flourished ever since. First, it was the Lin-ji form that was introduced by the Japanese monk Eisai (1141–1215 CE), who studied for a number of years in China. He is also famed for having introduced tea, which he greatly esteemed as a medicinal tonic. The Rinzai form of Zen had a strong appeal for the warrior class of feudal Japan, who found many of its methods congenial and compatible with their training as fighters. Though they became the main patrons of Rinzai, it was less popular in Japan among ordinary people, perhaps due to temperamental differences from the Chinese. It was left to Dogen (1200–1253 CE) to travel, in his turn, to China and from there to introduce the Cao-dong form of Zen into Japan. Together with Kobo Daishi, the great Shingon founder, Dogen is often considered to be one of the most outstanding thinkers that Japan has ever produced. His humanity and wisdom shine through every page of his magnum opus, *The Shobogenzo* (The Treasury of the Eye of the True Dharma). Like his Cao-dong predecessors in China, Dogen especially emphasized sitting meditation, as these words make clear:

Japan, due to its isolation, retained a more authentic form of Zen than did China.

The importance of tea-drinking in Japanese culture derives from the monk and Zen master Eisai.

SINCE THE ANCIENT SAGES SUCH AS SHAKYAMUNI AND BODHIDHARMA WERE SO DILIGENT
IN THEIR PRACTICE OF ZAZEN, HOW CAN PRESENT-DAY TRAINEES DO WITHOUT IT?
YOU SHOULD STOP PURSUING WORDS AND LETTERS, AND LEARN TO WITHDRAW AND REFLECT
ON YOURSELF. WHEN YOU DO SO, YOUR BODY AND MIND WILL FALL AWAY
NATURALLY, AND YOUR ORIGINAL BUDDHA NATURE WILL APPEAR.

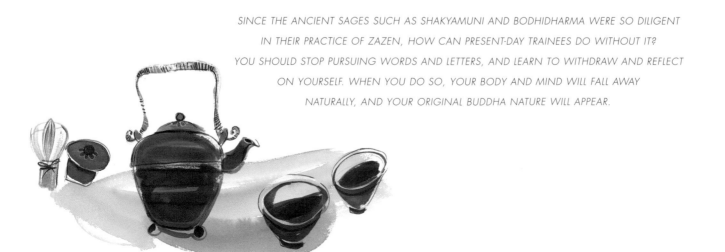

The Japanese built many beautiful temples, such as the Kinkakuji in Kyoto, seen here.

47

In Tibet, a form of Buddhism known as Vajrayana Tantric Buddhism, was adopted in preference to Zen. (Monks performing a ceremony at Ta Gong Monastery, Tibet)

TIBET

Zen Buddhist practice proved unpopular in Tibet.

Finally, a country that was not a Zen success story was Tibet. As Buddhism was being introduced into Tibet from India by some of the greatest contemporary scholars in the mid-eighth century CE, some Chinese Zen masters had also gained attention and support. The great Dharma king of Tibet, Tri-song De-tsen, was concerned about apparently conflicting doctrines taught by the Indian and Chinese parties. A great debate was held at Samyé Monastery between Kamalashila, the great scholar monk trained in all aspects of Indian Buddhism, and Hoshang Mahayana, a representative of the Southern School of Zen. The debate centered on the question of sudden versus gradual awakening and Hoshang Mahayana's claim that good works and other forms of personal development and study were unnecessary. A degree of political choice probably determined the outcome and Hoshang Mahayana and his Zen followers were trounced and ordered to leave the country. Later accounts from Tibetan sources make it clear that everything that appealed to the Chinese about Zen repelled Tibetan and Indian Buddhists and Zen made no further headway in Tibet, which instead adopted Vajrayana Tantric Buddhism.

The Tibetans were not the only people hostile to Zen practice. In China itself, there was hostility from such people as the Pure Land master Hui-ri, who spent seventeen years in India from 702 CE. His experiences with Buddhism there must have led him to criticize Zen masters on his return; he said they were arrogant, denied basic Buddhist teachings, misled people, and completely failed to develop compassion. Strong words! Although he also stressed the importance of sitting meditation, he condemned the teachings and practices of Zen. It is ironic, therefore, that Zen had to amalgamate itself with the Pure Land school in order to survive in China.

Monks chanting at the Jokhang Temple in Lhasa, Tibet.

ZEN IN PRACTICE

Chan, the original Chinese form of the word *Zen*, is a shortened form of the Sanskrit term *dhyana*. In Indian Buddhism, *dhyana* is one of the two main forms of meditation and refers to the training of the mind which leads to the ability to focus one-pointedly on any object it encounters. It was originally cultivated in order to stop the normal flow of thoughts and emotions. In this way, the mind was made free to penetrate

IF YOU WISH TO FIND THE BUDDHA,
FIRST YOU MUST LOOK INTO YOUR OWN MIND;
OUTSIDE OF THE MIND, THERE IS NO BUDDHA.
HAKUIN (1686–1769 CE)

beyond the superficial appearances of our everyday world. Unlike many other forms of Buddhism, it is the Zen view that only this will enable us to uncover our innate Buddha nature—no amount of study or even good deeds can achieve this. For this reason, the practice of this form of meditation is absolutely central to the practice of Zen Buddhism: it even takes its name from a word for meditation.

MEDITATION POSTURE

Since meditation is of central importance in Zen, it is hardly surprising that much attention is given to all its aspects. Although Zen practitioners will often spend some time doing walking meditation, it is seated meditation (*zazen*) that is most important. More than in any other form of Buddhism,

great stress is laid in Zen Buddhism upon the correct posture for meditation—in view of the great amount of time that a practitioner must spend seated. Initially, the recommended posture may be extremely uncomfortable, even painful, for the beginner. When a good posture can be maintained comfortably, this leads to certain benefits, such as calm and easy breathing, which in turn lead to a calmer and more tranquil mind free from disturbing emotions and thoughts.

Let us first look at the method traditionally recommended by Zen masters—which is still employed in Asian monasteries and temples. If you are doing your *zazen* in a temple or at a Buddhist center, the general

It is important to create a calm, peaceful setting for meditation.

environment should be suitable: clean and quiet with subdued lighting. When doing it at home alone, try to create a similar tranquil setting. To sit correctly, first you need to spread a large sitting mat on the floor—about thirty inches square and about two inches thick. Such mats are usually covered with a dark blue or black cloth, since brighter colors are distracting. On top of this mat, you should place a thick yet firm, round meditation cushion—normally about twelve inches in diameter. Be sure to wear loose-fitting clothing—possibly slacks, if you are a woman. You should then sit down in the full-lotus or half-lotus posture, placing the round cushion comfortably under your buttocks so that it tilts your hips forward. With your shoulders relaxed, you should place your hands in your lap, with your forearms resting on your thighs. Place your left hand on top of your right hand, with palms facing upward. Your thumbs should be raised and resting against each other. From the front view, the resulting hollow is traditionally said to resemble a wish-fulfilling gem with a wisp of fire at the top.

After you have settled down into position, you should sit upright with your back straight, leaning neither back nor forward. Hold your head up or incline it slightly forward. Your tongue should be placed lightly against your upper palate, with your mouth closed but relaxed. Your eyes should be partially but not completely closed, with your gaze directed to a point about four or five feet in front of you. When you are a beginner, you may fall asleep if your eyes are completely shut or you may be distracted by the sights around you if your eyes are wide open. When you are finally ready to begin your meditation session, you may find it helpful to sway once or twice to the right and left to settle yourself in comfort. This is the ideal physical posture for the practice of *zazen*—firm and unshakeable like a mountain.

However, for most Western people who are accustomed to sitting in chairs all of their lives, the full-lotus, or even the half-lotus, posture is virtually impossible, or soon becomes excruciating. For this reason, most Zen masters suggest various alternative sitting postures. A popular one, which has many of the advantages of traditional lotus postures, is the so-called tailor or Burmese style. For this, sit on the round cushion as before and simply bend your right leg to the left and place your left leg in front of it. Alternatively, you may want to try one of the low meditation stools that are easily obtained from specialist suppliers or provided at your meditation center. If all else fails, and you find it impossible to sit in any of these ways, you can sit on a chair of the right height so that your feet are firmly planted on the floor. Take care not to slouch back so that you are leaning against the back of the chair, as this will hinder your breathing and may lead to backache.

Many Westerners find the traditional lotus position (zazen) difficult to maintain.

BREATHING

When starting to meditate, you should breathe naturally and slowly and your breathing should not be artificially modified.

Virtually every single Buddhist tradition in Asia utilizes the breathing process as part of meditation practice but, unlike certain forms of yoga or Tantric meditation, the breathing process is not artificially modified in any way. It is sufficient to breathe naturally and slowly through your nose rather than your mouth. Inhale and exhale from the lower abdomen, shifting your center of gravity downward to your belly. You will find it helpful to do a couple of deep but slow inhalations and exhalations before settling down into your natural breathing rhythm. Now you are ready to begin your *zazen* training.

COUNTING THE BREATHS

The different schools of Zen that still survive in East Asia favor several different techniques of *zazen* practice, according to whether they are affiliated to the Soto or Rinzai lineages. Of these, the Soto style is closer to the standard form of meditation practiced throughout Asia, and so we shall look at this approach first. Once you are seated comfortably and have settled down, the first stage is the calm observance of the process of breathing. This technique is wonderfully simple yet profound in its effects. As you inhale and exhale, you should merely count

the breaths as they go in and out. It is usual to count from one to ten and then restart, all the while focusing on the area below your nose, where the breath flows by. This sounds very simple, but the beginner will very soon find that his mind has wandered off on a meandering journey of its own, following various trains of thought. As soon as you notice that this has happened, you should gently bring your attention back to the breathing process. You should not worry unduly about the flow of thoughts at this time; just relax and let go of them. Through repeated practice, you will gradually find that you are able to maintain your concentration on the breathing for the full count of ten.

FOLLOWING THE BREATHS

If you make good progress, your mind will slowly become calmer and more settled, with fewer distractions. As this happens, your breathing will also undergo changes: it will become slower and fainter. This phenomenon is well-known in other forms of Buddhism, hence Tibetan masters teach that the breath is the steed upon which the mind rides. As the breathing becomes more subtle, so also do distracting thoughts and emotions. As this begins to happen, it will no longer be necessary to count the breaths, for you will be able to become totally absorbed in the breathing process itself. During this time, there will no longer be any question of who is doing the breathing; it is no longer you who are watching your inhalations and exhalations. As you let go of the everyday mind, you will find that the process just happens by itself, no longer with any sense of separation between the part of you that is watching and the process itself.

ALL-ROUND AWARENESS

The final phase of *zazen* practice using this method moves you on to a state of pure and alert awareness. In Japan, this is known as *shikan-taza*, i.e. "nothing but sitting with alertness." This is the highest form of meditation in Zen and may take many months, or even years, of dedicated practice to achieve. Although beginners need to have some object to focus and concentrate their minds upon, such as their breathing process, this form of *zazen* transcends all focal objects. If you have diligently practiced the counting and awareness-of-breathing forms of *zazen*, you will have seen that your mind will gradually go beyond the normal division into a watching subject and watched object. It is difficult to give instructions for this level of *zazen* through a book, although it is possible to offer some hints about the experience itself.

Rather than focusing on any object at all, the aim of *shikan-taza* is a state of all-round awareness. When starting on this level of practice, your teacher may suggest that you initially imagine a sphere of pure awareness surrounding you. You are aware of yourself and all that surrounds you, you register the presence of these things, but are not distracted for one moment by them. One powerful image for this state is the mind of a warrior engaged in a duel with swords and faced by the possibility of death. Virtually no thoughts arise and even those that do disappear like bubbles of froth. In this state, the intrinsic clarity and radiance of the mind shines forth, unclouded by the normal rush of disjointed thoughts and emotions. In this way, you come into contact with your pure nature, your primordial face that is Buddha nature. Such is the energy generated by this form of intense concentration, your body will give off great warmth, and you may even find afterward that you are dripping with sweat. Although Tibetan yogins specifically cultivate this state for hours on end, it is not recommended that you remain in this state for too long in the Zen tradition—perhaps no more than thirty minutes at a time. You should take a break then, and switch to walking meditation.

WALKING MEDITATION

Walking meditation is known in Japanese as *kinhin*, although the style of doing it varies according to whether you are following the Soto or the Rinzai tradition. The Soto approach basically involves a mindful slow-motion walk around the meditation hall, whereas Rinzai practitioners move much more quickly and energetically. In Japan, the hands are clasped in front of the chest; the precise manner will be shown to you by your instructor, since there are several different ways of doing this. The Chinese and Koreans, on the other hand, walk with their arms hanging loosely at their sides. Regardless of the specific style of walking, however, you should continue with whatever meditation you were doing while seated—counting your breaths, silently following them, or meditating with all-round awareness. This change of physical activity acts as a break and helps to keep you alert while not disturbing the mental state you are cultivating. Once the walking meditation session has ended (after about ten minutes) you should seat yourself as before and continue with your *zazen*.

Walking meditation helps to keep you alert, while not disturbing your state of awareness.

KOANS AND MONDO

The Rinzai form of Zen has adopted a completely different approach to practice and emphasizes the use of the cryptic phrases or paradoxical stories known as *koans*. Although primarily associated with the Rinzai tradition, some use is made of *koans* by Soto masters, while Soto-style, objectless meditation is sometimes practiced by those taking the Rinzai approach. Though these *koans* have echoes in some forms of Tibetan Buddhism, they are basically an entirely new Chinese innovation in Buddhist practice. Many *koans* derive from the enigmatic question-and-answer dialogues known as *mondo* that took place between famous masters and their students. Many of these became so famous that they were preserved in several large compilations, such as the *Blue Cliff Records* and the *Gateless Barrier* collection. Famous examples include the following:

A MONK ASKED TUNG-SHAN, "WHAT IS THE BUDDHA?" TUNG-SHAN REPLIED, "THREE POUNDS OF FLAX." A MONK ASKED JOSHU, "DOES A DOG TRULY HAVE BUDDHA-NATURE OR NOT?" JOSHU REPLIED, "MU."

A monk asked Tung-shan, "What is the Buddha?" Tung-shan replied, "Three pounds of flax."
A monk asked Joshu, "Does a dog truly have Buddha-nature or not?" Joshu replied, "Mu."

Whether derived from earlier *mondo* or other sources, there are said to be about 1700 *koans* that survive today, although only about five hundred of these are in use today by Rinzai masters. Those *koans* still in use are graded, and are used as a way of measuring a student's progress by the degree of insight and realization that he or she can muster as a "solution" to the paradoxical or even nonsensical punch-line of the *koan*.

洞山和尚、因僧問、
山云、麻三斤。
如何是佛。

THE ROLE OF THE *ROSHI*

The Zen master, or roshi, leads the student through the stages of learning, step by step, and provides guidance and inspiration.

Although the role of the teacher is indispensable in all forms of Buddhism, the Zen master or *roshi* plays a key role in the training of Zen students. As well as monks, many *roshi* in the past were laymen and, indeed, some *roshi* in modern times, especially in the West, are women. Though standards are lower than in earlier times, a *roshi* is expected to have gained a high degree of realization following many years of training. The role of the *roshi* is to provide guidance and inspiration for his or her students, sometimes acting gently, sometimes harshly. Although a *roshi* is obviously important in the Soto lineage, the role is vital in the Rinzai tradition, which uses *koans*, since it is the *roshi* who applies constant pressure on his students and evaluates their progress.

APPLICATION TO *KOANS*

After a relatively short introduction to meditation technique, a student is introduced to one of the basic *koans*—in Japan, this is typically the famous *"mu"* dialogue quoted on page 59. In this example, we must remember that it is a basic tenet of Zen that all things, including dogs, are endowed with Buddha nature. On the face of his reply, Joshu seems to be denying this, for the word *"mu"* means "there is not" or "nothing." Yet this contradicts the belief in the universality of Buddha nature, and therein lies the problem. Instead of focusing on the flow of the breath, as in Soto, Rinzai students concentrate on this conundrum during meditation sessions. Periodically, they will be called for an interview with the *roshi* to give their understanding of the problem. Initially, they will resort to various ploys: they may try to solve it intellectually or use various theories they have picked up in their studies. These days, the worst a student can expect is for the *roshi* to shout angrily at them for their stupidity, but, in the past, violent blows with fists and sticks were commonplace. And so it goes on day after day, the *roshi* applying unrelenting pressure and the student becoming more and more desperate. For any hope of success, it is traditionally said that a student must cultivate three things to resolve a *koan*: great faith, great determination, and great doubt.

Eventually, after having exhausted all rational or discursive answers, the mind of the student makes a breakthrough. Transcending his everyday mind, the student cuts through the false and delusory veil of conceptual thought which conceals the underlying wisdom of inherent Buddha nature. In a flash, a unique answer bursts forth which demonstrates the student's realization. Then the process begins again with the next *koan* in the graded set, and so on, until the *roshi* is satisfied that the student has truly achieved awakening. When applied authentically, there is no doubt that this technique is extremely powerful and produces startling results. However, it is a sad reminder of the modern age to hear that there are *koan* "answer books" readily available in Japan and elsewhere. The low standards of many so-called *roshis* nowadays allow students to get away with such pointless cheating.

When the Zen student's mind can transcend everyday patterns of thought, true understanding can burst forth.

THE FIVE GROUPS OF *KOANS*

In the Rinzai tradition *koans* are graded into five groups. The first group are known as *hosshin* or Dharma Body (Dharmakaya) *koans*. These are the initial *koans* that a beginner will be asked to solve, and act as a means to introduce the student to the first experience of his or her intrinsic Buddha nature and the non-dual, unified nature of all phenomena. Next, there is the *kikan* or "support" group of *koans* which are intended to help the student perceive distinctions within their non-dual experience of reality. Then there is the *gonsen* ("pondering words") group, which is concerned with the profound content and significance of the sayings of past masters in order to make a student transcend superficial concepts and definitions. This category is followed by the *nanto* ("difficult to pass through") group of *koans* which, as their name suggests, are extremely difficult to resolve satisfactorily. Finally, there is the *go-i* ("five degrees") group of *koans*. The "five degrees" refer to the five levels of realization established by the master Tung-shan, and concern the mysterious interaction and interpenetration of the relative everyday phenomenal world and the absolute true nature of reality. When a student has mastered all five groups of *koans*, he or she has not finished training, but must learn the practical application in daily life of such realizations.

RESULTS

Whether a student follows the Soto or the Rinzai tradition, certain significant illuminating events will occur in the course of their practice and their interaction with their *roshi*. These moments are known as *kensho* ("seeing Buddha nature") or, popularly, as *satori* ("awakening"). Strictly speaking, *kensho* refers to the initial awakening to Buddha nature that a student undergoes early in his practice. Some books refer to these experiences as "enlightenment," but this is misleading; certainly no other Buddhist tradition would consider them as Enlightenment, for that implies full realization of Buddhahood. In Zen, on the other hand, one may, and indeed will, need to repeat the experience of "awakening" or realization many times—each refining the previous one.

Nevertheless, *kensho* represents a profound state of realization that cannot easily be described in words. Even the component parts of the terms "seeing" and "nature" can be misleading since, strictly speaking, there is no duality involving one who sees and that which is seen. Rather, it refers to a non-dual state wherein the primordial unity of seer and seen, subject and object, is experienced. The attainment of this state is said to prevent a practitioner from sliding back into the ordinary mental state of unaware people, and can provide the basis for further and more profound insights into the nature of reality.

NEGATIVE EXPERIENCES

Apart from healthy experiences of Buddha nature under the guidance of an experienced *roshi*, occasionally hindrances—traditionally known as *makyo* (diabolic phenomena)—may be encountered. These include strange hallucinatory sensations, visions, sounds, and even levitation. It was known long before Zen developed in China that the type of meditative concentration particularly favored in Zen can give rise to various types of supernormal phenomena and powers. Some of these are not intrinsically negative and, indeed, are actually sought in forms of Tantric meditation, but there is a danger that they will distract the practitioner from their development. It is possible that the word *"ma"* (devil) here refers to the Buddhist diabolic tempter called Mara. Mara is said to create various delusions and hallucinations in order to distract or frighten people from making progress on the Buddhist path. At a deeper level of understanding, Mara represents all things that might turn one away from progress and lead to spiritual death. As such phenomena arise, a skilled *roshi* will help his students deflect these negative experiences and focus their minds on the path.

As well as these strange phenomena, the chief obstacles that a Zen practitioner encounters are rather more mundane. For the beginner, sitting still in the approved position will often become excruciatingly painful; as each second passes, it becomes harder and harder to focus on one's breathing or the *koan* at hand. In particular, your knees and ankles will become painful, and then numb, though the return of sensation later can be just as painful. If the pain persists for some time after finishing the meditation session, then it is advisable to experiment with another posture. Any discomfort that is short-lived is not so important and may have more to do with your frame of mind at the time. Normally, you will find that the discomfort decreases as the months go by and you become accustomed to sitting still in meditation.

If there is no significant discomfort, another obstacle may arise: sleepiness. As in all forms of meditation, your mind should be alert and focused when doing *zazen*. Again, if you are not genuinely fatigued, sleepiness may be a sign of a certain frame of mind or problems with posture.

Traditionally, practitioners are told to remind themselves of their aims and intentions, thereby giving new impetus to their practice. Additionally, it is a good idea to check your posture, since a slouched and bent back quickly impairs breathing and leads to sleepiness. In contrast to this sleepy dullness that we experience sometimes, there is its opposite: a fidgety restlessness in body and mind. When this happens, we are distracted by the least thing: we have an itch, a pain, there is a noise outside, we feel hungry, and so forth. Our minds flit back and forth from one thing to another, we begin to daydream or make plans—all this conspires to prevent us from concentrating on the task at hand. Here, the antidote is patience and determination; everybody finds it difficult, at first, to relax and concentrate on breathing or a *koan*. Yet, as time goes by, we find that we are able to detach ourselves from our restless minds and we become more like observers, merely noting the rise and fall of our thoughts and emotions. Eventually, even this flow of mental events slows down and we become calmer and better able to focus our minds one-pointedly with relaxed alertness.

Formal *zazen* sessions in Japan are punctuated by the loud thwacks of a long paddle-shaped stick about a yard in length called a *kyosaku*, literally a "wake-up stick." This stick is used to help students overcome some of the obstacles mentioned above, such as sleepiness or lack of concentration. If the meditation supervisor's eagle eyes notice that you are dozing off, he will tap you on the shoulder with the *kyosaku*. You should then lean forward to receive two or three sharp blows across the shoulders or back. After they have been administered, you should bow and then you can resume your meditation afresh. The *kyosaku* is not used as a punishment, but to help the practitioner make progress, and some students will, in fact, signal that they want to receive it. As well as stimulating the circulation, it is said that the use of the *kyosaku* can even precipitate an experience of *kensho* when applied at the right moment. Viewed in this way, it is a modest version of the staff often used by Zen masters of old in China, with which they beat their students in an attempt to trigger a breakthrough into states of understanding beyond the everyday mind. The *kyosaku* is rarely used in the West. A less painful alternative, when you are drowsy and find it difficult to focus your mind, is to try the slow walking meditation.

*Buddha's fight against
the diabolical forces
of Mara, the tempter.*

Taking part in group meditation can be extremely beneficial for your own meditation practice.

GROUP MEDITATION

When beginning Zen meditation practice, it is vital to seek guidance. In most cases, this will mean joining a group that is meeting regularly at a center or temple. In the West, Zen has become very popular, and so it should be possible for most people to find some kind of group center within traveling distance. Even if you participate only once a week, this supervision will be invaluable, since meditation has many pitfalls awaiting the unwary. Taking part in group meditation is also beneficial, since it gives encouragement to the beginner, while applying a useful degree of pressure. Larger centers may well have a qualified *roshi*, or at least a senior student, in residence who can help with problems.

The hall where *zazen* is practiced is known as a *zendo*, and certain rules of etiquette apply, according to what tradition and lineage of Zen you follow. In general terms, those affiliated to Japanese lineages tend to be much more formal in procedure. Before you enter the *zendo*, you will have to remove your shoes, and so it is advisable to wear clean socks! As you enter, you should join your palms in a *gassho* and bow, for the *zendo* is a sacred space. Making your way to your allocated cushion, you face it, make another *gassho* gesture, and bow, because your cushion symbolizes the search for your Buddha nature. Finally, you turn away from your cushion and make another formal bow to your fellow practitioners. After this, you should then take up your meditation posture. When the session has finished, students of many Zen lineages also make another formal bow to their fellows again. In bowing to those around you, you are showing them respect by bowing to their intrinsic Buddha nature.

In the West, there are now many Zen groups who meet regularly for meditation in a temple or Zen center.

67

*Before meditating, ensure
you are in a calm, tranquil
area where you will
not be disturbed.*

PRACTICAL ZEN: ZEN MEDITATION

The correct meditational posture is highly valued in Zen practice, because when mastered it allows the mind to become settled more easily. Arrange your cushion on the mat in a quiet room where you are unlikely to be disturbed. For many Western people unaccustomed to sitting on the floor, it is quite difficult to fold the legs in the traditional lotus position, but an alternative can be used. Most people should be able to sit in the so-called Burmese style, first bending their right leg and then placing the left leg bent in front of it. Relax your shoulders and place your hands, palms upward, on your lap—first the right hand and then the left one on top of it. Your thumbs should be raised with the tips touching. Settle yourself into the position, while ensuring that you are not leaning off-center, to either side, backward or forward. Do a few long inhalations and exhalations to calm yourself a little before starting the meditation. Then focus on a point about five feet in front of you, with your eyes half-closed.

If you are a complete beginner, you should focus on the passage of your breath as it flows, keeping your attention on the place where you can feel the movement of air just under your nose. Count each inhalation and exhalation until you have reached ten, and then repeat the practice. You will soon notice that your attention has wandered away from your breathing. As soon as you do, just return your attention to your breathing and start the counting again. If you find it very difficult to keep your attention on breathing around your nose, try focusing on the rise and fall of your diaphragm. This is easier because there is greater movement in this area and also because you will probably find that you become calm and stabilize more easily. Try to do a minimum of thirty minutes of meditation, but no more if you are a beginner. When you come to the end of the session, open your eyes and stand up slowly.

ZEN IN DAILY LIFE

Though much time is spent in silent meditation, Zen practitioners are also encouraged to live their lives according to certain precepts and to apply the insights they gain through meditation to everyday situations. Merely to meditate without also putting other Buddhist teachings into practice in your daily life leads to a selfish dead-end which prevents further spiritual development. Mahayana Buddhism emphasizes the unity of

REFRAIN FROM WHAT IS EVIL,
CULTIVATE THE GOOD,
PURIFY YOUR MIND:
THIS IS THE TEACHING OF THE BUDDHA.

insight and compassion. Insight without compassion results in a cold-hearted disregard for the sufferings of others, while compassion without insight is often ineffective, since it is not possible to see what is truly needed by others. Both elements need to be developed simultaneously for you to experience any real understanding. The image of a chariot illustrates the situation: there is progress with the two wheels of compassion and insight, while we just go around in circles with only one wheel.

BEGINNER'S MIND

Zen writings often speak of the need to retain a beginner's mind. All too often, we make some progress with our meditation and gradually we begin to think that we know all that there is to know and are more advanced than others. We lose our freshness and enthusiasm, instead becoming stale and closed-minded. But qualities associated with the mind of a beginner are highly prized in Zen practice, so it is important not to lose them.

When we start as Zen practitioners, we are full of childlike excitement and enthusiasm. We apply ourselves to everything we are told to do with innocent single-mindedness, in the hope of making speedy progress and perhaps gaining our first experience of *satori*. Even when obstacles arise, we try to overcome them with wholehearted application to our meditation. But, as time goes by, and we do not seem to be making as much progress as we had originally expected, we begin to lose heart and perhaps find excuses why we don't need to meditate quite so often. A subtle invasive laziness pervades our minds and drags us down. Yet we should remind ourselves that the path of Buddhism is always uphill; if things are going all too smoothly without any struggle, then something is probably amiss. We should always remind ourselves of the Buddha's last words: strive with diligence!

Rather than losing heart in the face of difficulties, we should keep in mind that the path toward Enlightenment is always uphill.

The lucidity gained through meditation can help to enrich our relationships with others.

If we have made a little progress with meditation and we find that our minds have become a little calmer, we should try to bring this newfound tranquillity and clarity to bear upon our interactions with the people and situations we encounter from day to day. Normally we are tossed about in a maelstrom of conflicting emotions that govern the way we act and react to things. We are hostile to things and people that annoy and threaten our tender egos; we grasp and become attached to things that hold out the false promise of happiness; or else we act with narrow-minded prejudice and stupidity toward anything that is unfamiliar and cannot be easily pigeonholed into our preconceptions. Many of the qualities that we can bring to our lives from meditation will weaken these defensive ego strategies, so at times we must expect to feel uncomfortable in this new mental landscape without all of the familiar landmarks.

We can use the skill of bringing our attention to any situation with an intense single-mindedness, just as we have learned to be focused when we meditate. We are training ourselves to concentrate our minds on one object at a time; we are also cultivating the Zen virtue of wholeheartedness. So when somebody demands our attention, we do not deal with them superficially while wishing that we were doing something else. Instead of a halfhearted attitude, we find that we become progressively more able to give all of ourselves to them. If we focus our unwavering attention upon the situation at hand, or upon a particular person's needs, we may also notice that we are better able to see how we can help them or what lies below the surface. This is because the mind that has been disciplined by meditation is somewhat more lucid, being unclouded with our usual emotional reactions and flitting thoughts. This clarity of mind is said to lead to direct perception, where we can see things as they truly are. When this happens, our relationships with others are immensely enriched, for, without the usual fog of ego defenses, we can for the first time be truly intimate and open with others as adults.

When we operate in the world with our minds untrained by meditation, we encounter many unpleasant or disturbing things that we try to blot out from our thoughts. According to Buddhism, this is how the ego reacts when it encounters any changes that seem to threaten its comfortable delusions; it adopts various strategies from its rich arsenal of defenses. As we have seen, these will typically include anger, attachment, jealousy, pride, laziness, and greed. All of these defense mechanisms hinder the spontaneity that is so prized by Zen masters. Fortunately, it is not too difficult to discipline the mind, so at least the most obvious manifestations of these negative emotions can be controlled, and even eliminated. In particular, we can learn not to be confrontational in our dealings with others. In the modern urban world, there seems to be a rising tide of aggression and rage as we are confronted with many situations where we seem powerless to make things go the way we want them to go. But, when we have gained a degree of calmness, we gradually notice that we can deal with these situations more skillfully. In fact, if

Once we take the plunge into accepting the change and flow of life, we will experience less pain and unhappiness.

we are angry and hostile toward the world, we notice that we seem to attract more negativity from those around us, thus setting in motion a vicious cycle of paranoid suspicion. Bringing the lessons learned through meditation into our everyday lives tends to simplify our relations with others. When we see the nature of situations as they truly are, we realize that we have no need to react with hostility; indeed, if we inject single-minded attention and concern into our dealings with others, we also find that a little rubs off onto them.

Another benefit of Zen practice is a growing realization that all things are really impermanent and constantly changing, as the Buddha taught. If everything is so ephemeral, it is folly to attempt to hold onto what will inevitably slip from our grasp, no matter what we do. It takes great courage to go out into the world with openness and acceptance of the natural flow of life, for our normal reaction is an attempt to pin things down and freeze the moment so that it is safe for us. Though difficult at first to have enough faith in ourselves—like taking the first plunge in a pool when learning to swim—it is surprising how much less pain and unhappiness we experience if we do not cling and hold onto situations, people, or objects. As we gradually learn to let go, again letting a fresh spontaneity guide us, we also find ourselves being less judgmental about things. Normally we make a rapid series of evaluations and choices at each moment of our waking lives: this is good, this is bad, I want this, I don't like this, and so forth. The accomplished Zen practitioner does not do this, for he or she intuitively sees the nature of a situation and acts in the best possible manner, even when an inconvenient outcome turns out to be the result.

Finally, and perhaps most importantly, a Zen practitioner learns to be self-reliant. At the very outset, the Buddha taught that people should seek the truth for themselves rather than blindly following what others say. Some religions teach that you will be saved only if you believe in this or that, or that you must act in some particular way because God or the scriptures command you to do so. This is alien to Buddhism, for it teaches that the final arbiter of truth must be yourself. This is why the Buddha said that he did not want people to follow his path out of respect for his authority, but only if they tried out the teachings for themselves and found them to accord with reality. In Zen, the value accorded to self-reliance also lies in another idea. According to many schools of Mahayana, we all have an inherent potential for Enlightenment, i.e. for becoming Buddhas ourselves. Indeed, some teach that we are already enlightened from the very start, with their concept of Buddha nature. All that distinguishes us from Buddhas is that our Buddha nature is concealed by a dense layer of negative emotions, thoughts, and false ideas about reality. As these are gradually removed through meditation, the purity and radiance of our inherent Buddha minds shine forth and act as an infallible guide to spiritual progress. In Zen, when we rely upon ourselves, we are relying upon our intrinsic Buddha nature.

If we can remove negative thoughts and delusions through meditation, our true Buddha nature will be revealed and will act as our guide.

7 5

ENTRY ONTO THE PATH

Such are the virtues that will gradually emerge as we apply our meditation experiences to our daily lives. In order to guide us on the path, Zen offers a simple yet structured framework, beginning with the formal acceptance of the Buddhist teachings known as "taking refuge." If all things in the world are deceptive and transient, then the things we normally hold onto in the hope that they will protect us from unhappiness are false refuges, for they cannot provide us with security and peace. The only things that are reliable are the Buddha, his teachings, known collectively as the *Dharma*, and the *Sangha*, the community of all Buddhist practitioners. They are rare and valuable in the cycle of our countless births and deaths and they are known as the Three Jewels. To become a Buddhist of any kind, it is traditional to recite the following verse three times:

> *I take refuge in the Buddha*
>
> *I take refuge in the Dharma*
>
> *I take refuge in the Sangha*

This is all one needs to do as a declaration that one has become a Buddhist. Normally, you should take refuge formally—in the presence of your teacher or *roshi*, who acts as a witness. You will be given a number of precepts to adopt as a means of regulating your life so that the possibility of major negative deeds is reduced. Sometimes you will also be given a Buddhist name that should serve to inspire you in your day-to-day practice.

The declaration of "taking refuge" in the Three
Jewels is part of the process of becoming a
Buddhist. Here, novice monks in Taiwan take
part in an initiation ceremony.

OVERVIEW OF THE PRECEPTS

Buddhism comprises a wealth of teachings which can be presented in many ways, according to the ability of the practitioner. Yet all of these teachings may be summarized under three aspects: moral training, meditative concentration, and insight. Though laid out in a list, they are all interrelated and may even be seen as different aspects of the same thing. They are like a triangle, for the presence of any two always presupposes the third. Zen followers lay particular stress on the meditative concentration that calms the mind. From this, they believe that insight into the true nature of reality will arise. When these two are present, then moral discipline should also be present. Each of the three items interlocks with the others and, as each develops and matures, the others also gain in strength. For this reason also, they should not be seen in isolation.

Traditionally, Zen followers talk of sixteen precepts that form the foundation of Zen moral discipline and ethics. Though other schools of Buddhism prescribe slightly different sets of precepts, they are largely concerned with the same topics. The sixteen precepts comprise refuge in the Three Jewels, the Three Pure Precepts and the Ten Great Precepts. We shall look at the second and third items in detail shortly, but first we should consider the nature of precepts in Buddhism. It is important to realize that these precepts have little in common with the commandments in theistic religions, even though they look superficially similar. In the case of Christianity, for example, God commands people to obey His rules, which have been revealed through scripture. If people do not obey these rules, they will be punished accordingly. As Buddhism does not accept the idea of a personal creator god who ordains what we should or should not do, its precepts

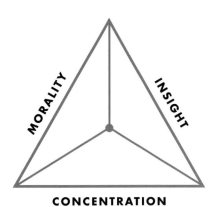

The three interrelated aspects of Buddhist teachings.

The Three Jewels:

Buddha

Dharma

Sangha

The Three Pure Precepts:

Cease all evil deeds

Cultivate goodness

Act for the benefit of others

The Ten Great Precepts:

Taking life

Stealing

Sexual misconduct

Lying

Use of intoxicants

Gossiping

Praising oneself

Meanness

Aggression

Slandering the

Three Jewels

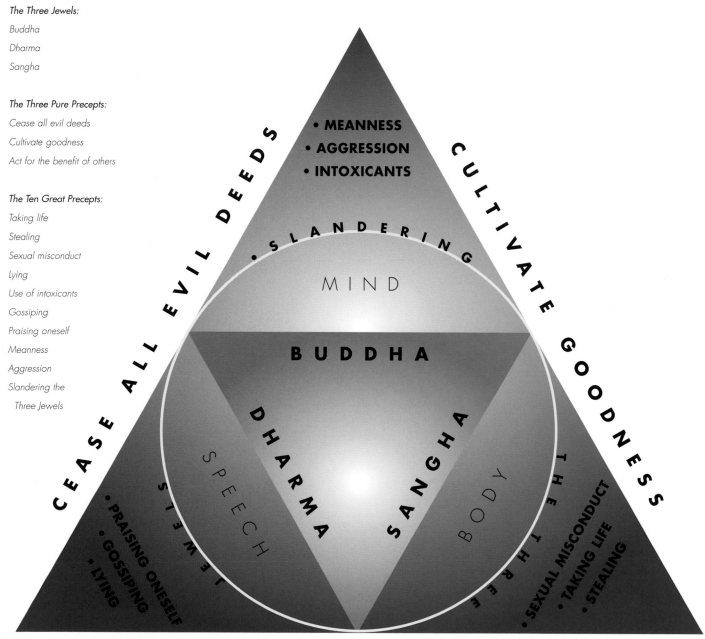

CEASE ALL EVIL DEEDS

CULTIVATE GOODNESS

ACT FOR THE BENEFIT OF OTHERS

• MEANNESS
• AGGRESSION
• INTOXICANTS

• SLANDERING

MIND

BUDDHA

DHARMA

SANGHA

SPEECH

BODY

THE THREE JEWELS

• PRAISING ONESELF
• GOSSIPING
• LYING

• SEXUAL MISCONDUCT
• TAKING LIFE
• STEALING

The Three Jewels, the Three Pure Precepts
and the Ten Great Precepts together form
the basis of Zen moral teaching.

are based on a different concept. For instance, the first precept concerns taking life. As Buddhists, we refrain from taking life not because somebody will punish us if we do so, but because it is damaging to our spiritual progress and causes suffering to another. Moreover, as trainee Bodhisattvas who are dedicated to helping other beings free themselves from the cycle of birth and death through a strong sense of compassion and kindness, such acts run contrary to the whole spirit of the Buddhist path.

THE THREE PURE PRECEPTS

Following refuge in the Three Jewels, Zen followers adopt a very old formula which sums up the entire Buddhist approach to morality and ethics:

Cease all evil deeds

Cultivate goodness

Act for the benefit of others

Though they sound very simplistic, these three lines encapsulate all aspects of daily practice. We need to cease, or at least refrain from, wrongdoing as far as possible, because negative deeds only bring us more misery and tend to cloud our true selves in murky spiritual darkness. To do good has the reverse effect and guarantees us a degree of happiness and peace, and makes our ability to apply ourselves to meditation easier. As a form of Mahayana Buddhism which especially emphasizes the welfare of others, we are urged to act at all times for the benefit of others rather than ourselves. By acting for the sake of all beings (not only human) around us, we further develop and express our true natures, while weakening the hold the false sense of ego-mind has on us.

Zen Buddhism has a positive view of human nature, for it teaches that all beings are primordially enlightened, and that the Buddha mind lies below the surface of everyday discursive thought and emotionality. When a beginner has made a degree of progress with meditation, flashes of this underlying nature shine forth spontaneously. Apart from bestowing insight into the dynamics of daily life, our inherent Buddha nature can act as a kind of conscience or guide to what is right and what is wrong. When sufficiently accomplished, perhaps after many years of practice, a Zen practitioner hardly needs to recite a formal list of precepts, for he or she can act spontaneously in the most appropriate and pure way in any situation.

Though of universal application, there is a kind of hierarchy in the set of sixteen Zen precepts. The Ten Great Precepts are perhaps for beginners as they give more specific guidance. As a practitioner makes progress, he or she can rely on a summary for guidance rather than having everything spelled out at length. At an advanced level, the Three Jewels are also like precepts, with refuge in the Buddha being the supreme and only precept from which everything else naturally flows. Since, according to Zen, we are already endowed with an enlightened Buddha nature, we should be able to trust our innermost instincts about our conduct and dealings with others, for Enlightenment is intrinsically compassionate, benign, and wise.

THE TEN GREAT PRECEPTS

Though the two previous sets of precepts are vital to an understanding of Zen morality and ethics, a beginner usually needs more explicit guidance. This is provided by the third group of precepts, known as the Ten Great Precepts. These can be listed briefly in the form of simple injunctions, but they contain many implications that will become apparent only after years of training and meditation. Put simply, these precepts forbid the taking of life, stealing, sexual misconduct, lying, the use of intoxicants, gossiping about the misconduct of others, praising oneself while deprecating others, being mean-minded with spiritual or material gifts, aggression, and slandering the Three Jewels. These are adopted by both lay practitioners and monks, although the latter should also maintain total celibacy. When first adopted, these precepts may be seen as restrictive commandments—don't do this, don't do that. It is difficult to see beyond the bare words of the precepts, and to realize that they also have positive implications which truly capture the spirit of Buddhist morality and ethics.

TAKING LIFE

Buddhism teaches that all life is sacred and should be protected and nurtured as far as possible.

When we are urged to refrain from taking life, this initially relates to killing other humans; however, most people nowadays will never be faced with such a possibility. Buddhists believe that all life is sacred because all living beings have Buddha nature, and we must refrain from killing any living creatures, whether for food, out of anger, or for pleasure. The destruction of life implicitly involves suffering on the part of the victim—suffering which we, as trainee Bodhisattvas, should be trying to alleviate rather than increase. We should endeavor to cultivate and encourage life in all its forms as far as possible. This means that we should not only desist from killing, but from all other acts which bring harm to others and to ourselves. Not only should we desist from killing and harming, but we should do all we can to prevent others from killing and harming, and not to condone any such acts in the world. One of the most destructive forces in human nature is violence, whether arising from hatred or mere stupidity. As such, it should be completely abhorrent to anybody, let alone a Buddhist. Thus, the true spirit of this first precept is to cultivate compassion and to protect or nurture life. It also implies that we should take care to conserve and protect our natural environment, resisting all attempts at greedy exploitation of natural resources.

STEALING

We should refrain from stealing and all other forms of theft. Traditionally, Buddhists have defined theft as the taking of anything which has not freely been given. This also includes more subtle forms of theft, such as the exploitation of others, and other forms of oppressive social injustice. We must learn to be more aware of the suffering and misery that any form of theft brings upon its victims. As there are many needy people in the world, we ought to be as generous with our resources as possible. If we have limited material possessions to share with others, we still have our time and energy, which we can place at the disposal of others for their well-being. This concern for the material and spiritual welfare of other beings implies the cultivation of loving kindness, one of the great Buddhist virtues. Not only should we cultivate generosity, while resisting all temptations to be dishonest, but again we should strive to prevent others from acting out of greed, or profiting from the suffering of other beings, whether they be human or other species.

Generosity to others can take many forms, including concern for their material and spiritual well-being.

SEXUAL MISCONDUCT

Along with the need for food and sleep, the sexual urge is one of the most potent biological instincts. As such, Buddhists see sexual functions as a part of the natural world, and not intrinsically wrong. However, since sexual relations are all too easy to abuse, the very power of these sexual urges can lead to extremely negative results which are in themselves a great source of unhappiness. Since loving kindness and respect for others form such a central element of Buddhist morality, we may say that the positive aspect of this precept implies that you should only enter into intimate relationships with others with love and respect. We need to learn how to act with responsibility so that we can protect both the mental and physical health of our partners. We should never engage in sexual relations without love and a long-term commitment to our partners. At the same time, we should not engage in any sexual activities which might destroy the relationships of other couples or families. Although many would class sexual abuse as a form of violence, which indeed it is, it also relates to this precept. For this reason, we should do everything in our power to protect children from sexual abuse, for we shall be party to the guilt and harm caused by it if we condone or turn a blind eye to it.

Although the sexual instinct is part of the natural world, we need to learn how to act responsibly and respectfully toward those we love.

LYING

We should always bear in mind the powerful effects of our words on others, and should speak truthfully and listen carefully.

All forms of dishonest or intentionally misleading communication are classed as lying in Buddhist terms. We often forget the power that words have, for they can bring about happiness or suffering. Remembering this, we should always speak with mindfulness, while taking care to listen carefully to what others are saying to us. Buddhists value honest, truthful, and loving speech very highly. It is said in some scriptures that a Bodhisattva should never lie, even if he might lose his life as a result. This precept covers a much wider range of concepts than merely refraining from lying. Our speech should inspire people with hope, joy, and confidence. We should take care not to gossip and spread rumors about others that we do not know to be true, nor should we say things that will cause discord and division. On the contrary, we should, through our example, try to bring about reconciliation and harmony in society. We should try to have the courage to speak out against injustice as far as possible, even though it might endanger or inconvenience us.

THE USE OF INTOXICANTS

Basically, any substance that clouds the mind and harms the body is considered to be an intoxicant. Since the aim of all Buddhists is to become enlightened by developing clarity of mind and insight, anything that hinders this process is deemed to be harmful. Apart from the more obvious kinds of intoxicants, such as alcohol and addictive drugs, we should also give consideration to the kind of food we eat. Too many types of food in modern Western society are unsuitable for a healthy lifestyle, especially junk food that is laden with additives, fats, and sugars. This burdens our bodies with toxins that affect our health and cloud our minds. Even if we eat only healthy forms of food, it is still possible to misuse what we eat through gluttony. The corollary of this precept is to cultivate good physical and mental health by being mindful about our diet.

The traditional diet in East Asian Buddhist monasteries is balanced and vegetarian, and it is prepared and eaten with mindfulness. We also should be aware that the consumption of certain kinds of foods involve violence and exploitation, and thus are linked with the precepts against killing and stealing. An even deeper level of understanding of this precept relates to various types of noxious mental foods that we may ingest— in the form of negative and corrupting television programs, books, and magazines, for example.

We should take care to nourish our bodies with a healthy and balanced diet—and our minds with wholesome "mental food."

THE REMAINING PRECEPTS

The previous five precepts form the core of Zen Buddhist morality; indeed, they are cultivated in all Buddhist countries from Sri Lanka to Tibet, as well as East Asia. The remaining five precepts can be seen as useful elaborations on these first five—perhaps making more explicit the things which we need to be careful about—therefore we can review them more briefly.

Gossiping about the misconduct of others obviously relates to the precept concerned with lying. It expands on that precept and reminds us not to engage in any gossip or frivolous talk about others, even if it is true. We should be more concerned about our own behavior than to criticize others unnecessarily. If we want to help somebody who is misbehaving in some way, it is better to do this quietly, in private, with compassion and understanding.

Instead of criticizing someone who is misbehaving in some way, it is best to help them quietly, in private, with compassion and understanding.

Just as we cannot judge nature, we should not be quick to judge others, for we cannot see the motives and intentions in their minds.

Similarly, we should not stoke up our own arrogance and pride while criticizing or deprecating others. On the contrary, we need to remain modest about our own achievements and abilities, while praising those of others in order to encourage them. We should not be quick to judge others, for we probably do not have the wisdom to see the motives and intentions that lie inside their minds.

Generosity is the cornerstone of a Bodhisattva's ethical training, through which compassion and loving kindness are developed. Thus, we should not be mean when we are called on to make spiritual or material gifts. First and foremost, poor people need material gifts, which we should bestow if we can without ostentation and pride. If we are unable to help much materially, there are two other gifts mentioned in the scriptures: security and the teachings of the Buddha. For instance, many people live with fear and anxiety, and we can help them if we are in a position to give them reassurance, which we should do in any way we can. The best gift of all is that of the Buddhist teachings, which should be given freely to all who care to listen. The Buddha himself particularly condemned the closed-fisted nature of some teachers who demand payment or other rewards for their knowledge.

By resisting any form of aggression or anger that may arise in our minds, we try to maintain equanimity in the face of all irritants that life may throw at us. Anger is said to be like a match applied to a great heap of straw; any goodness we have accumulated will be destroyed in an instant by it. Regular practice of meditation will help us to keep our minds calm and peaceful. This state of mind will reflect itself in our physical activities—we shall act calmly and patiently, taking care in all we do.

Finally, we must at all costs avoid slandering the Three Jewels. This means we should not slander, criticize, or even idly joke about the Three Jewels. If we defame the Buddha, the Dharma, or the Sangha, we are alienating ourselves from the very means by which we are seeking our own liberation and Enlightenment. Disrespect for the Buddha is worst of all for, ultimately, we are defaming our own Buddha natures, which can lead to our spiritual death. Instead, we should respect the Buddha, do all we can to spread the Dharma (the teachings of the Buddha), and provide sustenance for the Sangha (the Buddhist community).

Most of us will not infringe these precepts in a gross or major manner, but we should not be complacent because of that. Indeed, it is the steady, insidious accumulation of small faults that defiles our minds and prevents real progress. Perhaps it is for this reason that somebody once said that great sinners make great saints. However, if we find that we have failed to uphold any of these precepts in some way, we should also not become too despondent, for we are still beginners. There is no god in Buddhism who is going to punish us for our failings; at worst, we shall experience a degree of resultant unhappiness or suffering that we bring upon ourselves. The best thing to do is to acknowledge our shortcomings sincerely and make a firm commitment to avoid them in the future. Perhaps we should reflect on the reasons that led us to break the precept. An understanding of our motives and intentions is often the best way to make progress.

In honoring and respecting the Buddha,
we respect our own Buddha nature,
our own spiritual guide.

Zen practitioners aim to achieve
a sense of calm detachment
from the hustle and bustle of
everyday life, while remaining
keen observers of events.

PRACTICAL ZEN: DAILY LIFE PRACTICE

The aim of Zen practice is not to sit all the time, meditating, but to interact with the world calmly in the most appropriate manner. Normally our minds are filled with a rush of distracting thoughts and emotions that turn our attention away from the matter at hand. In this way, we can easily act in ways that are unskillful or hurtful to ourselves and others. Try to cultivate a sense that you are detached from the events around you, but intensely observing them. Think of the way that a cat will focus patiently, without any distraction, on the tiny rustle of a mouse!

It is not easy to achieve this state without long practice, so it is best to pick one area of activity to work on. If you are doing some housework, such as cleaning or cooking, try to approach it as though you were doing your meditation practice; instead of focusing on your breathing, focus on the matter at hand without letting other thoughts intrude. Similarly, if your attention wanders, gently bring it back to what you are doing now. If you are at work or socializing, try to watch how you interact with others. Are you aware of how your actions and words affect others, or do they just seem to happen?

The aim of Zen practice is to act spontaneously but, strange to say, this is done by first engaging in your actions with attention and mindfulness. Try to be aware of the half-hidden thoughts and emotions that prompt you to act the way you do. If you experience some sort of conflict with others, look dispassionately at your own motives. These usually lie hidden below the surface of your mind, but are the controlling power behind whatever you do. Try analyzing each step back from the action you were involved in, uncovering each layer of thought and motivation. You will find that disharmony usually occurs when you are prompted by these hidden but negative emotions and thoughts. However, recognizing them is the way to weaken their hold on you permanently.

Everyday activities such as cooking can be approached in the same way as meditation: with a single-minded focus on the task in hand.

ZEN AND HEALTH

The Zen way of life is all-encompassing. It does not concern itself only with the mind, but regards a healthy body as equally important. The realizations that are gained through formal meditation practice are put to use in balancing the body and mind in a healthy manner in daily life. The idea of intrinsic Buddha nature encourages the Zen practitioner to treat all of life with respect, beginning with his or her own body. This led Chinese Zen followers to adopt special yogic techniques and exercises designed to strengthen the body. They believed that a healthy mind is to be found only in a healthy body. Monks in Zen monasteries paid careful attention to a harmonious and nutritious diet that avoided unwholesome kinds of food. As Zen spread from China to neighboring Japan, it was further integrated into all aspects of daily life, and even the life of warriors, who were to learn to live with equanimity in the face of death.

WHEN IT'S TIME TO EAT, I EAT;
WHEN TIREDNESS COMES,
I SLEEP.
ZHAO ZHU (778–897 CE)

RELIGION AND HEALTH

The idea of practicing a religion or a spiritual path for its health benefits may seem strange and unfamiliar to many people in the West, but this is not so in Asia. Most of us are now familiar with hatha yoga, although we may not be aware that it is intended as the first stage of a profound path of spiritual development. As we shall see, a number of the more physical types of training done by Zen practitioners may well have developed from ideas introduced into China by Bodhidharma. One reason why the connection between religious training and health seems unfamiliar may lie in the traditionally dualistic idea people in the West have concerning the relationship between the body and the mind. It might be said that the underlying attitude that we have inherited from early Christianity is that the body is imperfect or even evil, while the mind and spirit are potentially good. The body is a nuisance and, like the natural world, is to be disciplined and controlled so that it does not interfere with our religious life. This hostility toward the body has its roots in the Gnostic sects which were popular during the early years of Christianity, and, although they were deemed to be heretical by the early Church Fathers, some of those ideas crept into and pervaded Christianity. In contrast to this, Eastern religions, including Buddhism, do not consider the body to be intrinsically bad, although basic instinctive urges may need to be restrained at times. On the other hand, Buddhism also recognizes that many aspects of physical sickness arise through negative emotions and thought processes.

While Western thought is fundamentally dualistic, Eastern religions understand mind and body as intimately connected.

THERAPEUTIC CONCEPTS IN BUDDHISM

From its inception Buddhism has utilized a number of concepts and practices from traditional Indian medical science, so the occurrence of definite health benefits through the practice of Buddhism should not be too surprising. When the Buddha explained the Four Noble Truths, which were to become the cornerstone of his teachings, he adopted the traditional approach of a doctor to his patient. The first Truth, that there is suffering, is like the doctor's diagnosis of a sickness. The second Truth, concerning attachment, is similar to a doctor pointing out the cause of the illness. The third and fourth Truths are equivalent to the prognosis and the cure. In the same way, when the Buddha talks about negative or positive mind states and emotions, he does not say that they are evil or good, but that they are unhealthy or healthy, as the case may be. In this respect, the Buddha's approach is similar to that of a modern psychologist; he does not pass judgment on an individual's thoughts and actions by considering the person to be good or bad because of those actions, but says that some thoughts and actions are unhealthy and unskillful.

Buddhist practice, which involved aspects of traditional Indian medicine, can be therapeutic, both spiritually and physically.

MEDITATION FOR HEALTH

Though later on, in both India and China, various kinds of physical exercises and training were gradually introduced into Buddhism, its chief therapeutic method is meditation. Naturally, the aim of meditation in Buddhism is not specifically physical or mental well-being and health, for Buddhism is a religious path that aims at spiritual health through unfolding Enlightenment and directly understanding reality.

The popular use in recent years of meditation by Western doctors as a therapy, without the religious dimension, is a debased form of meditation. Although that use of meditation will bring about some benefits by promoting calmness and clarity of mind, it can hardly be considered to be the true use of meditation.

As we have seen, whether in Zen or any other school of Buddhism, meditation is like a tool that we use to examine ourselves and the world we inhabit. It is a way of arriving at the same experience of Enlightenment as the Buddha did himself.

When he became enlightened, the Buddha made a number of observations about the manner in which we bring about pain and unhappiness for ourselves through our basic lack of understanding of the dynamics of existence. We can look at some of the Buddha's insights and observe how they are utilized in meditation in order that we may bring about healthy changes in our daily lives.

Calming Meditation

There are two types of meditation in Buddhism, which may appear in different guises according to the particular school concerned: calming meditation and insight meditation. In the first form of meditation, the mind is focused on any wholesome and spiritual object, most typically the breath, to slow down and eventually suspend the normal flow of disruptive emotions and thoughts. When an individual can achieve a one-pointed state of concentration, the mind will become peaceful and clear, the breathing will automatically slow down and the body will experience great calmness. In Buddhist technical terminology, the body achieves a state of "workability"—which is characterized by relaxation, flexibility, and increased stamina. It is this form of meditation that is most often used by Western therapists, for the benefits are quite obvious. The central role of stress in the origin of many modern ailments, such as heart disease, some cancers, or stomach ulcers, is becoming widely accepted today, since it causes chemical changes in the body, raised blood pressure, disturbed sleep, and emotional disturbances. Even if not practiced as part of spiritual training, the benefits of calming meditation are considerable in counteracting these problems by reducing causal stress.

Insight Meditation

Although it is a form of meditation that is less well-known in the West, insight meditation is the means by which it is possible to make permanent changes in the practitioner's state of health and well-being. While regular practice of calming meditation has undoubted benefits, traditionally it is not thought to bring about permanent changes in an individual. In order to do this, the practitioner must apply the powers of attention that he/she has developed to examining the structure and dynamics of life itself, both on an individual and a universal level. The mind is normally unfocused and does not have the ability for sustained introspection, but jumps restlessly from one thing to another like a playing monkey. The stillness and clarity that are developed by calming meditation thus prepare the way for insight. It is said that the various negative traits that continually surface in our lives are like weeds; through calming meditation, we cut them back, but only through insight meditation can we permanently uproot them. The way we do this is to use certain key teachings of Buddhism that act as templates or models which assist us to see things differently. In other words, they help us to see why we think and act in ways which lead to spiritual, mental, and physical sickness. Often, just to see and understand what is happening within us enables us to abandon negative or unskillful traits. We shall look briefly at some of these meditation templates and what benefits they bring.

THE BUDDHIST VIEW OF THE INDIVIDUAL

The key feature of the Buddhist view of the individual is that there is no underlying permanent and independent self.

In many ways, Buddhist analysis of the individual in general, and specifically the mind, is vastly more sophisticated than current Western concepts. The key feature of the Buddhist view of the individual is that there is no underlying permanent and independent self. Rather, the individual's sense of self arises through the interplay of five constituent elements: the physical body, feelings, thought processes, motivation, and consciousness. Through insight meditation, we carefully and repeatedly examine each of these components of our being in an attempt to identify anything

that could be termed a self. As each of them is subject to change and alteration, none of them can correspond to a permanent self. Careful introspection, using these five components of our individuality, fails to turn up any element which could be deemed a permanent self. To be sure, Buddhists do not deny a conventional or empirical self—the self we refer to when we use our name or the pronoun "I" in everyday speech—but it turns out that there is nothing else present. However, ordinary people seem unaware of this and so cling firmly to a belief in a real ego-self. This illusory ego-self is the source of much dysfunctional behavior in daily life, which can lead to mental and physical sickness.

THE WHOLESOME AND UNWHOLESOME EMOTIONS

The illusory sense of a real ego-self encompasses a wide range of unwholesome factors. Once we are convinced we *are* a real ego-self, we develop a whole range of negative or unwholesome motivational strategies in order to avoid anything that seems to threaten our cozy illusion. These motivational strategies become so ingrained that we normally fail to see them for what they truly are, and perhaps think that there is not much that we can do about them in any case. As a meditational tool to enable us to examine these processes at work, the Buddha identified a large set of unwholesome attitudes, together with their wholesome counterparts. Using this set to identify and label our various attitudes as they arise and come into play is vital if we are to have any hope of freeing ourselves from them. For example, when our ego-self feels threatened and fearful in any way, it predictably reacts in one of three basic ways. It may attempt to drive away and reject the source of discomfort through anger and hatred or, alternately, it may try to smother and control it through greedy attachment. If neither of these ploys seems appropriate, the ego-self tries to ignore the situation and pretend that nothing is happening, by way of a self-imposed stupidity. From each of these three major coping strategies, a host of subsidiary or derivative factors arises.

With insight meditation, we try to identify all three ego-self reactions as they arise, watching the dynamics of the situation that lead us to react in these ways. Before long, we come to see these reactions for what they are: unnecessary devices to protect something that does not really exist in the first place! If we are able to do this, we can then begin to learn how to modify our behavior that flows from these negative attitudes and thereby reduce the likelihood of damaging or destructive actions that can ultimately lead to unhappiness and suffering. The same process also works with wholesome attitudes; we can identify what it is that empowers us to act beneficially, both toward ourselves and toward others, and can thereby take steps to foster such positive mental postures.

ZEN

Since all things are interconnected, nothing occurs by chance or in isolation: the events in our lives form part of a vast web.

INTERDEPENDENCE

When the Buddha became enlightened, he later told his disciples that central to this achievement was a realization that all things are interconnected, that nothing occurs by itself or without reason. In other words, things do not happen to us as individuals by chance, but always through a complex web of conditions and causes. We have just seen how this relates to the dynamics of our personal lives, in connection with the arising of negative attitudes. This process can be deepened still further. We can examine the process by which each of the five component elements of our individuality interact and give rise to all of our experiences, we can observe how a faulty understanding of the dynamics at work leads us to a belief in a real ego-self, and so forth. In addition, the concept of interdependence is useful as a means of overcoming our usual sense of separateness as the power of the ego-self delusion wanes. Much unhappiness in the world arises from the feeling that we are alone and solitary, standing against all else. In contrast, the Buddhist view, especially emphasized in Zen, is that we are all interconnected and equal in value. This helps to create a sense of harmony between ourselves and others and promotes a real sense of joyful peace. It enables us to open ourselves to the world around us, free from the fears that normally beset us. We begin to see how it is our own unskillful attitudes and behavior that cause conflict and friction with the people with whom we have dealings. In this way, Buddhism helps us to cultivate a sense of personal responsibility, for we begin to understand that we ourselves play a key role in what befalls us.

MINDFULNESS

Although most people need to cultivate the skills involved in insight meditation through formal sessions, mindfulness can and should be applied in all situations in which we find ourselves. Being mindful means that we look dispassionately at ourselves and our activities. When we first start doing this, we tend to slow down so that we can observe what is going on. This in itself has profound implications for the physical health of most of us, living as we do in a busy urbanized society where we are bombarded with sense impressions at every waking moment. Another benefit is the way in which mindfulness forces us to focus on the present. Although Buddhism teaches that all beings are subject to rebirth through countless lives until final Enlightenment or liberation are reached, it also stresses the importance of the here-and-now. If we look at the thoughts that flash through our minds, we cannot help noticing that most of them are concerned about what we have or have not done in the past, and what we hope, expect, or dread will occur in the future. In other words, most of the time we are not *here*, but elsewhere. Mindfulness is a good technique for bringing us back to the present and thus minimizes the usual pangs of guilt and anxiety that can be so destructive and stunt our personal growth.

It is important to slow down and take the time to observe what is really going on in the present moment.

103

SPONTANEITY

It may seem strange to say that mindfulness is linked with spontaneity, but a little reflection will help us see why this is so. Zen Buddhists generally believe that there is a pure and creative element inherently present in all of us, which they term "Buddha nature." Needless to say, this is not the same thing as the delusory ego-mind, for it transcends the individual person and, at its deepest level, pervades the entire universe. However, this intrinsically present Buddha nature is concealed by a thick veil of confusion and negative attitudes. As we practice *zazen*, we begin to cut through this mass of obscurations, and our true nature spontaneously shines forth. As we gain experience with *zazen*, we are able to give the same kind of intense attention to all that we do, whether walking, sitting, talking, or working. When we are no longer distracted by the rambling thoughts we are usually plagued with, we can see situations more clearly for what they are, and also intuitively see the best way of dealing with them. If we do not operate from a false sense of ego-self, we no longer need to use the various stultifying coping mechanisms that we have developed over the years, and so we are able to act with greater spontaneity and creativity. What starts out as a somewhat contrived process of mindfulness eventually becomes second nature and allows us to act more freely than we could have imagined possible.

When we learn to cut through the illusions of the ego-self, our true Buddha nature will shine forth spontaneously.

THE POWER OF THE MIND

Centuries of experience with meditation have allowed Buddhists to predict the occurrence of certain unusual phenomena. Western psychologists are ill-equipped to understand or explain these manifestations, and may indeed try to dismiss them as pathological delusions, even though they are well documented throughout Buddhist history. However, the development of powerful concentration, which arises through the practice of *zazen* or other forms of meditation, leads to various mental powers, known as *joriki* in Japanese, which seem almost supernatural. These arise due to the continuous state of awareness which is cultivated through mindfulness. Mindfulness enables us to act spontaneously in situations where most people would fall back on familiar stale patterns of behavior. A corollary of this spontaneity is the ability to act in any situation, no matter how unexpected or difficult, in the most appropriate manner. Bystanders looking on might be forgiven if they thought some supernatural power was at work, but in fact the phenomenon is quite natural. Additionally, various powers that are well known to Tantric adepts in the Tibetan Buddhist tradition also emerge through the practice of Zen. These include various paranormal abilities such as clairvoyance, clairaudience, and certain types of telepathy. I shall not dwell on these; all meditation masters discourage excessive interest in these powers, for there is a real danger that students may become sidetracked and seek out such an ability as an end in itself and, therefore, fail to make further progress toward Enlightenment.

PHYSICAL HEALTH

As Zen developed in China, it adopted and incorporated various ideas and techniques from Taoist practices. Underlying these practices is the concept of *qi*, a term that literally denotes the air, breath, or energy, but is understood to be the "vital energy" or "life force" that pervades all things. Control of this primordial energy was one of the main goals of religious Taoism in its search for longevity and even immortality. The Taoists developed various exercises aimed at controlling and regulating the breath in order to strengthen and increase *qi*. If this is done successfully, major physiological changes occur that enable the body to achieve a high degree of health and to perform extraordinary actions. In this respect, the concept of *qi* is similar, if not identical, to the role of *prana* in India. Although Buddhists in India and elsewhere did not originally concern themselves particularly with breath control in meditation, later forms of Buddhism adopted such techniques that must have formed part of the common religio-medical culture of their society. Some basic techniques were probably known to Buddhist monks from the earliest times, and were practiced as a means of maintaining their health.

SHAO-LIN KUNG FU

Bodhidharma found that the monks at Shao-Lin Monastery were too weak to sit for long hours in meditation. To help them cope, he taught them two sets of physical exercises. These were developed and transformed into the more complex techniques that have been transmitted for hundreds of years at the Shao-Lin Monastery. Bodhidharma probably brought these methods with him from India. Traditionally, it is believed he taught the Eighteen Arhat Hands and Sinew Metamorphosis. The Eighteen Arhat Hands is a set of gentle and graceful movements that developed into the Eighteen Arhat Fists—the basis of kung fu. Sinew Metamorphosis, a more forceful technique for manipulating the flow of *qi*, forms the basic principles of the Shao-Lin *qi gong* methods. These exercises are not intrinsically Buddhist but they embody the desired qualities of Zen practice. To engage in Shao-Lin kung fu effectively, students must unify their mind, breathing, and movements. At the outset of a session, you usually visualize the cosmic energy flowing down through your body and out of the feet into the ground, thus transforming the individual into an integral part of the universe.

ZEN AND THE MARTIAL ARTS

Some people are surprised that Zen was adopted as the spiritual component of several forms of martial art in the East. It is not that Zen practitioners specifically developed martial arts themselves, but that those who were warriors or fighters in the past in China and Japan found much solace and benefit in Zen teachings. The physical aspect of the martial arts requires the same single-minded concentration that is stressed by Zen Buddhism. Faced with the possibility of instant death, the warrior cannot afford to be distracted, but needs the all-round awareness that comes through years of diligent *zazen* training. Any combat situation involves a complex flow of energy, so if a warrior has learned to attune himself with the world around him by subduing the functioning of his ego-self, the resulting state of harmony ensures a good chance of survival in combat.

On a spiritual level, the Zen element in the martial arts teaches the combatant to act with both compassion and dispassion. When you encounter aggression and anger, it is all too easy to lash out in retaliation. A Zen training allows you to respond in an appropriate manner, often to the extent that conflict can be avoided completely.

In medieval Japan, the ideal among swordsmen was not the sword that kills, but the sword that saves. In his younger days, the famous swordsman Minamoto Musashi took his battered sword to be sharpened and cleaned. He was shown by the swordsmith a sword belonging to another swordsman that did not have a mark on it—truly the sword of a Zen master. Musashi did not understand at first when the swordsmith told him that it belonged to a truly great swordsman, but later he learned that the supreme skill is not to kill but to save lives. In other words, the sheer spiritual presence of a Zen-trained master swordsman was sufficient to avert violence. Certainly anger and hatred had no place in the mind of such a warrior for, although he may have been required to fight somebody, he would always have been aware of that person's Buddha nature. In my own experience, those who have trained in martial arts such as aikido and kung fu are, in fact, generally compassionate and gentle people who show great self-control and strive to defuse violent situations if at all possible.

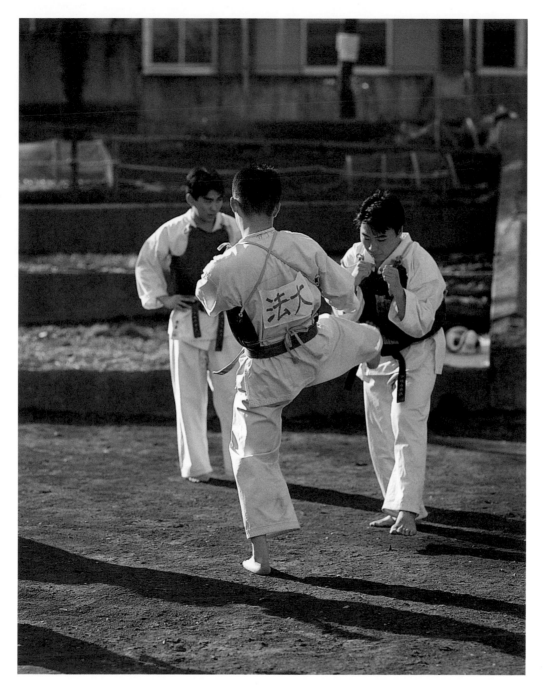

*The all-round awareness
produced through Zen training
is an important aspect of martial
arts such as aikido and kung fu.*

ZEN AND FOOD

Buddhists believe that all beings reincarnate until they are enlightened and freed from the repeated cycle of life and death. Taken literally, this means that any animal may well have been a human in a previous lifetime—even your own close relative. To kill animals and eat them for food, then, becomes a form of cannibalism to be avoided at all costs. In addition, Zen Buddhists believe that all beings, not just humans, are intrinsically endowed with Buddha nature and therefore deserve respect. For this reason, they have usually eaten a healthy vegetarian diet. Moreover, the love of nature and simplicity led them to prefer a simple diet of wholesome food—what we would now call organic food. It was prepared without elaborate flavoring and decoration, and certain foods (in addition to meat) that were known to cause physical disharmony were avoided. The typical diet in Zen monasteries of the past closely resembled the macrobiotic diet that has become popular in recent decades in the West. The basis of the macrobiotic diet itself was developed by Taoist monks, but was adopted by Buddhist monks for its health benefits.

Food should be prepared with mindfulness, love, and respect. Rice, for example, is carefully washed, and stray pieces of chaff and other impurities are removed. Cooking is done attentively, and food is presented to those who are to eat it as though it is a devotional offering. In Japan, great care is taken with the aesthetic qualities of the bowls and plates. In the days before refrigeration, only vegetables that were in season could be used, but they were carefully chosen so that their colors would be pleasing to the eye. Before the food is eaten, prayers are usually said dedicating the meal to all buddhas, and to remind you that the meal serves as nutrition for the body and mind so that Enlightenment may be swiftly realized. While it is being eaten, silence should be observed so that full attention can be given to each well-chewed mouthful. This level of mindfulness in the preparation and eating of food also serves to remind people of their interconnectedness with the natural world and thus fosters a sense of harmony and peace. This attitude to food is much needed in the present age when many people eat convenience food that has little nutritional value—something we recognize when we call it "junk food."

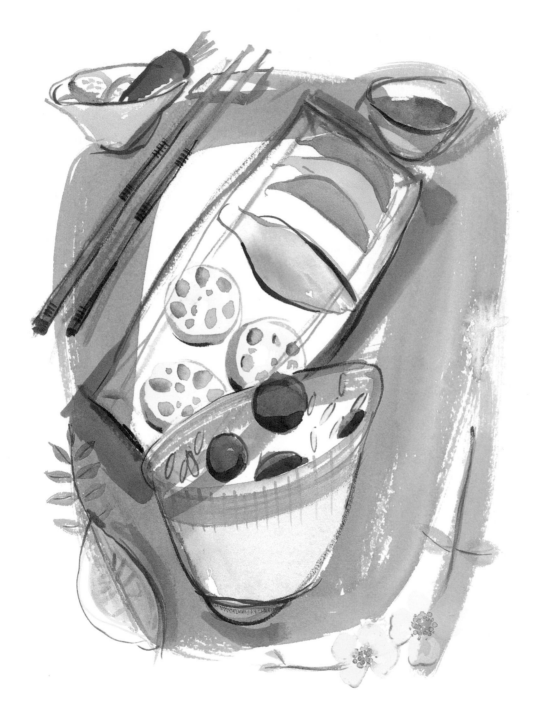

Zen Buddhists usually eat
a simple vegetarian diet;
food should be prepared,
served, and eaten with
mindfulness and respect.

111

Many forms of martial arts, such
as archery, can be incorporated
into Zen practice and can aid
the cultivation of mindfulness.

PRACTICAL ZEN: THE MARTIAL ARTS

*Focus your attention on the target,
clearing your mind of all distractions.*

Zen was attractive as a philosophy and as a way of life for the warriors of medieval Japan. Even today, there are many martial arts forms that can be incorporated into Zen practice. The key to using the Zen technique in martial combat is first a total unity of mind and body, and then total integration with the environment. The first step is to take your meditation out of the shrine room and to cultivate mindfulness in daily life. The more you become aware of your own particular patterns of behavior, the less likely you are to be caught by surprise by a sudden flare-up of emotion. For a warrior, any such outburst—of anger or jealousy, for example—is potentially fatal. No matter how dynamic your actions need to be, you will find that you are aware of each phase of your movements so long as you maintain mindfulness.

Traditional archery is still practiced in Japan by many men and women, and, though the equipment is somewhat different, a similar approach could be taken with Western archery. Take up your position in front of your target with the bow at your side. Breathing calmly, focus your attention on the target for several minutes, free from all distractions. Then smoothly raise the bow and place the arrow in position. With one gliding movement, draw the bow to its full extent, all the time keeping your attention on the target. Do not think about hitting the target, but, without premeditation, release the arrow. Even if you fail to hit the bull's-eye, remain calm and gently lower the bow. Relax and try again. The technique for combat with another person is similar—focus your attention fully on the movements of the other person and do not allow yourself to be distracted by anything else happening around you. If you are able to fix your attention fully on your opponent, you will remain unruffled and able to sense his or her moves as they are about to happen.

ZEN AND THE ENVIRONMENT

From the time of the Buddha onward, care and respect for the environment has been stressed by Buddhism. As Buddhism spread to China and Japan, this love for nature resonated with native aesthetic feelings, and found its greatest expression in the art and architecture of those

WHAT SHALL BE MY LEGACY?
THE BLOSSOMS OF SPRING,
THE CUCKOO IN THE HILLS,
THE LEAVES OF AUTUMN.
RYOKAN (1758?–1831 CE)

countries. Though we may be unable to recreate in our twentieth-century Western homes the kinds of structures and gardens that were so influenced by the great Zen masters of the past, we can at least emulate their constant striving for harmony and simplicity. Many aspects of Japanese Zen design can be seen in avant-garde architecture and the currently popular minimalist interiors. While many people who have arranged their dwellings along these lines are unaware of the origins of these influences, modern Western followers of Zen can emulate certain elements of the Zen style in their homes for the spiritual value which they impart.

THE PLACE OF HUMANKIND IN THE WORLD

A great rift exists between the monotheistic religions that originated in the Middle East and the religions developed in India and the Far East, which has resulted in different views about the place of people in the world. The monotheistic religions set humankind apart from the rest of the world with all of its plants, animals, and natural features. There seems to be an implicit, or sometimes explicit, idea that God created the world and everything in it for the benefit and use of humankind. Furthermore, human beings are viewed as different in value from all other living things:

In Buddhist thought, humans are not seen as superior, but as an integral part of the natural world, on a par with all other creatures.

only humans have "souls," only they will be saved or enter paradise. The model for the human position in the world is derived from the relationship of God to his creation. Just as God is the overlord of the entire universe, so also in a limited way has humankind been granted dominion over the world—it is there to be used and exploited. The outcome of this can be seen all around us; the destruction and exploitation of the natural world, based on greed and convenience, with little surviving religious influence to restrain the worst excesses.

In the East in general, but specifically where Buddhism is practiced, the situation was, until recently, very different. There was no polarization between humankind and all other creatures—they were all considered to be on the same level. Humankind was not set apart from nature, but was an integral part of it.

This idea is derived from several key concepts in Buddhism. Perhaps most significant is the idea that no god created us, and the world, for our benefit, but rather that all things arose together, and are inextricably intertwined through the workings of karma and interdependence.

Though many people nowadays do not take the Buddhist teachings on rebirth literally, this was not always the case. The reality of rebirth, according to the quality of one's karmic actions, meant that an individual might be reborn in any one of a number of possible modes of existence. Traditionally, six levels were taught in Buddhist scriptures: the proud gods, the jealous demi-gods, the lustful humans, the benighted animals, the greedy hungry spirits, and the hate-filled denizens of hell. The effects of particular types of actions, positive or negative, accumulated through your life, and determined which one of these states would be your next home upon rebirth. Needless to say, the effects of karmic actions are not permanent, so, when the energy that resulted in any particular type of existence has been exhausted, you are reborn yet again—perhaps in a better, or worse, state. Given that this is the case, it is quite likely that everybody has, at some time or other, been born and lived as an animal, and that every animal has at some time been human. The upshot of this is simply that a human has no strong grounds for supposing that he or she is superior to other life-forms—although there may be some temporary advantages.

THE SANCTITY OF LIFE

From the earliest times, Buddhism has held very benign views about the value of life. Naturally, in common with all the major religions, Buddhism teaches that taking life is evil. Where Buddhism differs is that it says the taking of any life—not just human life—is wrong. The Buddha recognized the destructiveness of violence and killing not only to the victims, but also to the perpetrators. To harm the life of another being intentionally is seen as the best way to guarantee a rebirth in hell, while depriving the victim of opportunities to find liberation and happiness.

This strong ideal of compassion that is found in Buddhism is described throughout countless

Since all living creatures are endowed with Buddha nature, they are all to be respected as potential buddhas.

scriptural texts—e.g. the self-sacrificing nobility of the Bodhisattva who puts his or her comfort and happiness beneath that of others. Bodhisattvas constantly strive to improve the lot of others, so how could they even consider any action that brings about harm?

This feeling of commonality and love toward all living beings was further strengthened by later developments in Buddhism that were to be particularly influential on Zen practitioners. The explicit expression of the idea of Buddha nature was pivotal in leveling all living beings, for all are endowed intrinsically with Buddha nature. That is, all beings are potential buddhas and, since it is the greatest of sins to kill a buddha, then it is equally wrong to kill a being who is potentially a buddha. For this reason, abstention from meat-eating was stressed in later Buddhism, although it was implicit even in its earlier forms. To eat the body of another creature was viewed as a form of cannibalism and the popular idea grew up in China among Zen practitioners that everything in the natural world—even plants, trees, and the very rocks—partakes in this same Buddha nature. In the eyes of Zen practitioners, all of nature is sacred, and equal in value, from an absolute point of view. All natural things should be respected and nurtured as far as possible, rather than exploited and slaughtered for selfish human ends.

For Zen practitioners, all of
nature is to be respected and
celebrated, including the trees,
the plants, and even rocks.

119

The solitude and tranquil beauty of a mountain setting can aid spiritual development in the Zen disciple.

ZEN AND THE MOUNTAINS

The Buddha spent much of his life after Enlightenment teaching townspeople the *Dharma*, but also spent much time in remote and secluded parts of the countryside. Many meditation manuals praise the solitude to be found in the wilds far from the bustle of everyday life. To develop efficiency in the one-pointed concentration so vital to successful meditation, the trainee is urged to withdraw from the world into the mountains. Such texts dwell on the natural beauty that can be found in such places: the craggy vistas with caves for shelter, the streams of fresh water, the sounds of birds and other wildlife, the splendor of the trees and flowers. The language used shows a high degree of appreciation for the tranquillity and harmony that can be enjoyed by the recluse who chooses to live there. These texts seem to be saying that, for spiritual development, a person's true home is in the midst of an unspoiled natural environment. It was in this spirit that many of the great Zen masters, such as Hui-neng in China, wandered among secluded mountain regions to polish their insights. It was well known that this desire

A DAY WITHOUT WORK
IS A DAY WITHOUT FOOD.
BAI-ZHANG (720–814 CE)

to leave the bustle of urban life can sometimes lead to escapism and apathy toward the suffering of other beings, so life in such places was recommended for trainees. Once they had achieved a high degree of detachment, meditative stability, and insight, however, they were urged to return to the world of people to help and teach them.

At first the Zen school in China did not have its own monasteries, as many of its followers engaged in an itinerant lifestyle, wandering about the countryside and into the depths of the mountains. However, as the fame of the Zen masters grew, they gathered large numbers of followers around them. Their somewhat unorthodox and iconoclastic views meant Zen masters were often unwelcome at the large monasteries that were affiliated with the older established forms of Buddhism. As we have seen, the patriarch Dao-xin established the first Zen monastery at Mount Shuang-feng in the seventh century CE in response to the need for monasteries dedicated to the Zen way. Though many Chinese monasteries and temples had been built in mountainous regions in the past, virtually all the early Zen monasteries were built thus, far away from urban centers.

MONASTIC ARCHITECTURE IN CHINA

Over the centuries a great number of Buddhist monasteries have been destroyed, either by natural causes or deliberately by war and persecution. In some cases they were rebuilt when the situation was favorable, but that was not always the case. For this reason, a history of Buddhist architecture in China must remain incomplete.

When Buddhism first entered China, its temples and monasteries were invariably located in the great cities, where they acted as showcases for the new religion, centers for the translation of texts and their dissemination, and, above all, for worship and pilgrimage. Only later did the number of Buddhist establishments increase throughout China, often constructed with the patronage of wealthy local people.

Curiously, most Chinese religious architecture is identical and follows a traditional design both in layout and structure. Until you enter the monastery or temple, it is often difficult to tell whether the place is Confucian, Taoist, or Buddhist. According to the importance of the establishment, it may be large and well-decorated or rather more modest and plain, but, overall, there is a great similarity between them.

Buddhist monasteries in China comprise a collection of separate buildings—often built of wood, or sometimes stone, or even brick—with gracefully bowed tile roofs, all laid out to form a rectangle. Typically, a monastery has one large main hall which acts as the focal point of the place, with its main statuary of the Buddha and provisions for worship, with several side halls housing statues of lesser Buddhist figures. Nearby are living quarters for the monks and facilities for their daily life such as the kitchen, storerooms, bathhouse, and latrines. The whole assembly of buildings is enclosed by a high wall pierced by a splendid main gate. These buildings usually have a stone base upon which huge timber pillars are set to support the elaborate eaves and heavy, tiled roof. The walls are made of timber planks and latticework, or an infill of materials such as stone and brick.

ZEN MONASTERIES

The Zen school constructed their own monasteries, but they did not leave any lasting influence on the architectural style of the buildings, for the building tradition in China was extremely conservative; what was found to be suitable for the climate and the availability of materials continued to be used for centuries. Yet there are some differences to be noticed. Built as they were in remote areas, Zen monasteries were seldom centers of pilgrimage at the

Zen monasteries tend to be simple and unelaborate—places for serious work rather than display.

outset, and so were less ornate than those in the large cities. This simplicity was partly out of necessity, due to lack of funds, but it also represented the Zen preference for the simple and unelaborate. An excess of decoration was thought to be extravagant, unnecessary, and likely to distract the Zen monk from his quest for Enlightenment. In other words, a Zen monastery is a place for serious work—not display. One difference between the Zen monasteries in China and others elsewhere was the provision of a multipurpose hall, said to have been introduced by Bai-zhang. The purpose of this hall was to provide a place where the monks could sleep, eat, and meditate without moving from their straw mats, thereby encouraging the monks to focus all of their efforts and attention on Zen practice when not working in the fields or workshops.

ARCHITECTURE IN JAPAN

Since Buddhism was introduced into Japan from China, apart from some small input from Korea in the sixth century CE, it should not come as a surprise to see that Buddhist architecture in Japan has taken many cues from its Chinese ancestors. Indeed, a number of early Chinese-style buildings have survived in Japan, so the history of Chinese architecture must make reference to the ancient temples and shrines of Japan. However, what eventually emerged as the most characteristic style of building in Japan skillfully blends native tastes and materials with some elements of Chinese architecture.

When the Japanese first made contact with the culture of the mainland, their own buildings were probably constructed along the lines of the Shinto shrines that still exist throughout the country. These single-story buildings have unpainted wooden walls, surrounded by an encircling veranda, and are covered with a thick thatched roof. Variations on this theme can still be seen in the old farmhouses that dot the more remote parts of the country, although the thatch on the roof has often been replaced with blue, galvanized metal sheets. Even the older town houses, fast disappearing, have the raised floor and veranda. To some degree, these buildings would be recognizable to the earliest founders of the Japanese nation.

Shinto shrines, like this one in Kyoto, are usually constructed from wood, with a veranda and thatched roof.

THE *SHINDEN* STYLE

Impressed by everything Chinese, the Japanese in the eighth and ninth centuries CE introduced many aspects of Chinese culture—writing, the legal system, the hierarchy of social structure, religion, medicine, and building styles. During the Heian period (794–1185 CE), temples and vast aristocratic palaces or mansions were built with a strongly Chinese flavor. While the very early temples, such as the Shitennoji in Osaka, are almost indistinguishable from the Chinese models, these slightly later buildings do make some concessions to Japanese tastes and requirements.

The style of building most typical of the Heian period is called the *shinden*. These vast complexes of structures were often built within the confines of the capital, and yet some were almost as large as country estates. They were dominated by a single large dwelling flanked by secondary structures connected by narrow, covered passageways or galleries open at the sides. Internally, there were no permanent walls to provide seclusion; when privacy was needed, curtains or hinged partitions were moved into place. Just as their Chinese models, these *shinden* were roofed with heavy, glazed tiles supported with elaborate painted gables and eaves rather than the indigenous thatching, and their walls were constructed of plaster-coated clay rather than wood. The visible parts of the structure's upright and horizontal timbers were painted vermilion.

Although Zen influence is often seen in various aspects of Japanese culture, it is likely that much of what is called Zen is merely the traditional Japanese sense of aesthetics. For example, what is considered a typical Zen-inspired love for simplicity and nature seems to have been present from the earliest days in Japan. Thus, the *shinden* had virtually no internal ornamentation, and furniture was extremely meager. Though some were imported as luxury items in the Heian period, carpets never became popular in Japan, and are not even to this day. Unlike the equivalent Chinese dwelling, the Japanese did not use chairs or couches, but sat on thick floor mats of woven reeds and straw (*tatami*) that could be moved around as needed. Indeed, from the earliest times to the present, all daily activities in Japanese dwellings have been carried out at floor level—whether they are sitting, eating, or sleeping.

Japanese interiors, as in this Shinto shrine, are usually simple and uncluttered, with a minimum of ornamentation.

*A Shinto shrine
on Hokkaido, Japan.*

KAMAKURA AUSTERITY

Since this form of architecture retained many features from its Chinese counterparts, it stands out as somewhat alien to Japanese culture, even in its modified form. It was only later that there was a return to the earlier taste for natural and unadorned materials. Nevertheless, the sense of fluid internal space and openness that was found in the *shinden* building style was to remain a feature of all Japanese architecture. After the fall of the Heian era and the start of the warrior-dominated Kamakura period (1185–1333 CE), considerable changes were seen in building styles. The Kamakura warrior aristocracy was well disposed toward the newly imported Zen, for it seemed to accord with their own austere warrior ideals. This interest in Zen can also be seen in the architecture of the time. The typical kamakura dwelling changed from the sprawling grandeur of the *shinden* with its detached galleries and passageways. Ever conscious of the need for security in the wake of a long civil war, the Kamakura style of building compacted all of the necessary elements of a dwelling under one roof. The somewhat gaudy external decoration of the *shinden* was abandoned, and the structural timbers were left in their natural state to weather and mellow into a silvery gray. Internally, the large open spaces were sectioned off with the heavy, sliding, paper-covered partitions known as *fusuma* that are still used in Japan. In this way, rooms were created, each with its own purpose.

ZEN INFLUENCES

The popularity of Zen among the ruling class of warriors in Japan continued even after the end of the Kamakura period. Many of these warriors were all but illiterate at that time, and consequently employed Zen monks as scribes. For this task, the monks needed a place for writing, so a kind of desk, known as a *shoin*, was provided for them in the form of a window alcove with a raised sill, usually looking out over a small garden. Since this is where the resident Zen monk did his writing, a place was also created to store scrolls, paper, and writing equipment—a wall cabinet set into a niche. Both this cabinet and the *shoin* were directly modeled on similar arrangements to be found in Zen monasteries in Song dynasty China. These study rooms were typical of quality buildings at the time, and the buildings themselves were given the generic name of *shoin*.

These arrangements soon became status symbols for the new ruling class, and consequently became the focal point of the house, where important guests were entertained. A further Zen feature was introduced—an alcove along one wall called a *tokonoma*, where flowers or objects of art were displayed with simplicity. It is interesting to note that the *tokonoma* in Chinese Zen monasteries was more of a shrine than a display alcove; it was the place where Chinese monks burned incense and contemplated religious artwork. The *tokonoma* is still a standard feature in all Japanese homes, even when they are twenty floors up a ferroconcrete tower block!

By the sixteenth century CE, a mixture of native Japanese aesthetics and Zen innovations had created most of the features that we now associate with the typical Japanese house and temple. While the *shoin* had been the house for the warrior elite, the simpler version known as *sukiya* became the model for ordinary people. It retained many of the features of the *shoin*, but on a less grand scale, and became the form of the traditional Japanese house in the following centuries. Like the larger *shoin*, it used *fusuma* to define the internal rooms, and its floors were covered from wall to wall with blocks of thick *tatami* matting. The strength of these buildings derives entirely from the structural timber uprights and horizontals, so the outer walls serve no other purpose than to keep out the elements—to a degree. In direct contrast to the stone or brick walls of Western houses, these walls are simple, sliding, lattice frames (*shoji*) covered with semi-translucent paper.

The alcove, or tokonoma, used for displaying religious artifacts or art objects, is still found in many Japanese homes.

LANDSCAPED GARDENS IN CHINA

The influences of Zen aesthetics and a love of nature can be seen in the gardens that surround monasteries, temples, and secular dwellings. Long before Zen had become popular in China, large landscaped gardens were to be found encircling the great palaces and many of the well-endowed monasteries. These gardens may have originated in the Han dynasty (206 BCE–220 CE) when the emperors sought the location of the five paradisical Isles of the Immortals, thought to lie off the coast of Shantung. When they could not be located, one emperor hit upon the idea of creating a rival paradise in the form of a beautiful landscaped garden on his estate, which would so please the Immortals that they would take up residence there.

Whether the Immortals took up the offer or not, this idea of the landscaped garden as a model of the heavenly paradise persisted in China in later centuries. When Buddhism had put

In China, landscaped gardens, such as these Yu Gardens in Shanghai, were originally intended as models of the heavenly paradise.

down roots and was supported by the nobility, they saw their gardens with their lakes and islands as symbols of the paradise of the Buddha Amitabha, popularized by Buddhist Pure Land teachings. At the same time, religious Taoism was growing in influence, and gardens also began to reflect its love of the mountains. If gardens could not be located so that they had a backdrop of distant mountains, then large boulders and rocks were piled up on islands in these gardens to represent mountains. This Taoist influence persisted into the Tang period and later, leading to a greater emphasis on the untamed rugged qualities of mountains and streams in many landscaped gardens. The development of cultural links with China during the Heian period led to the construction of the first Japanese gardens— around the palaces and mansions of the aristocracy and royal family. The Japanese were no doubt attracted to the idea of gardens not only because gardens were impressive status symbols, but also because many elements of the Chinese garden resonated with the Japanese love of nature.

LANDSCAPED GARDENS IN JAPAN

At first landscaped gardens in Japan had little religious significance, for they were more like private pleasure parks, filled with lakes and islands, where the idle aristocracy could indulge themselves in various refined pastimes. Unfortunately, few of these gardens survive in Japan, since most were long ago destroyed, although the ancient garden of Mozuji in northern Japan still provides some idea of their appearance. With the overthrow of the Heian aristocracy by the Kamakura warriors, there was an accompanying shift in garden styles. The rulers commissioned several large gardens, not for their own private use, but attached to temples. Religious symbolism returned to these landscaped gardens, for they too were designed as models of Amitabha Buddha's Pure Land paradise.

Zen monks from China introduced the simple, nature-loving style of garden to Japan. (Leaping Tiger Gardens, Nanzen-ji Temple, Kyoto)

Around this period, Zen Buddhism was being introduced into Japan by monks such as Eisai and Dogen, who had seen the Song dynasty style of landscaped gardens. Like the architectural changes occurring in Japan around this time, the gardens reflecting the Song period delight in an artful simplicity and love of the natural environment. In contrast to the richly textured gardens of the preceding Tang period, the intelligentsia and nobility in Song China preferred a simple and unelaborate style. In many ways, this new taste merely reflects the often monochrome ink paintings of landscapes that are so typical of the Song period. It was this style of garden that Zen monks imported and further developed in Japan.

THE GARDEN AS A PAINTING

The Zen aesthetic stresses a sense of openness and space. We have already seen this in architecture but it is present, perhaps even more strongly, in the Japanese landscaped gardens that were constructed during the Kamakura and Ashikaga periods. Adopting hints from Chinese gardens of the same period, the Japanese Zen gardeners envisaged the garden as a kind of three-dimensional painting. Trees and shrubs of different sizes were used, and small lakes and streams created, while large, moss-encrusted boulders were carefully chosen to look as natural as possible—they were to be interesting to look at, but not too bizarre or outlandish, as was often the case in Chinese gardens. Their landscaped gardens uniquely made extensive use of perspective and foreshortening to create an illusion of space, even when the garden was small.

The Japanese "stone garden" uses rocks and sand to create an austere space for contemplation and meditation.

This was done in a number of ways—e.g. by planting trees and shrubs with large, light-colored leaves in the foreground, while placing those with small, dark-colored leaves in the background. Similarly, paths were made to meander across the garden, gradually growing narrower before they disappeared among trees to the rear of the garden. Rocks and stones were carefully selected and graded so that those in the distance were smaller and less distinct, while small streams wound around rocks and plants. Any walls or fences were completely disguised through the use of natural materials, and camouflaged by thickets of shrubs. The aim of the Zen gardeners was to create a beautiful environment that seemed to be entirely natural in origin—a garden to contemplate rather than to stroll around in, as had been the case with earlier gardens.

STONE GARDENS

Some examples of Zen landscaped gardens have miraculously survived, but many were destroyed during the ravages of civil war that devastated Japan during the fifteenth century. Many monasteries, as well as the mansions of the elite ruling class, were destroyed with their gardens. A mood of sadness and melancholy spread through Japanese culture at that time. It was during this period that Zen gardeners took the three-dimensional painting aspect of their gardens to its logical conclusion. Just as the Song dynasty landscape paintings were done with brush and black ink alone, a new style of Zen garden was created: the stone garden, using little more than sand and rocks. These gardens were truly religious in purpose—no longer were they designed for pleasurable strolls or even the contemplation of scenic beauty. Their sole purpose was meditative contemplation to promote an experience of the deepest truths of Zen Buddhism.

One of the most famous of these stone gardens is that at Ryoan-ji in Kyoto. With this rectangular garden, the size of a tennis court, we come in a full circle in one sense; an array of five groups of island-like rocks, set in raked, coarse white sand, echoes the early Han Chinese gardens. As with all such gardens, the rocks have been chosen with great care, for there should be no hint whatsoever of human intervention. Rather, the rocks should look like miniature versions of the great crags and mountains depicted in the ink paintings. These five groups of rocks are made up of different shapes and sizes that are carefully arranged asymmetrically. The largest group has five rocks, while two groups have three rocks, and two more groups have just two rocks. The larger groups are dominated by one larger boulder that rises above smaller ones which flank it. The sand is carefully raked every day to suggest waves—for no water is permitted within the stone garden style—running lengthwise with circles around each of the rock groups. This combination of raked lines and grouped boulders rising up creates a unique sense of dynamic tension. It also illustrates a basic Buddhist concept in a concrete manner: the open space of the sand suggests emptiness, while the rocks stand for phenomenal forms. It thus unites nothingness with existence in a non-dual manner—the very essence of Zen teaching.

It is possible to transform a Western garden into a Zen-style stone garden using rocks and coarse sand or gravel.

PRACTICAL ZEN: ZEN GARDENS

It requires years of training to create an authentic Zen style of garden. However, some features can be adapted to the West without great difficulty, apart from the time and hard work involved in rebuilding a garden. The stone garden that is so typical of Zen temples in Japan should, ideally, be constructed in a rectangular shape with the length at least one and a half times greater than the width, and with the long side running parallel to the viewing area. It should be surrounded on three sides with fairly high, solid, fences made of unpainted wood in its natural state, to block out extraneous views. It is also pleasing to place a line of dark, evergreen trees on the far side of the fence to frame the garden. The whole area should be cleared of plants and shrubs, and then carefully leveled so that there are no dips or bumps. You then need to set several groups of large rocks into the ground. These can be bought from large garden suppliers. Ensure that they are not smooth and polished. They should be somewhat rough, even a little jagged, and have clearly defined, natural striations and coloring for interest. In a small garden, two or, at most, three groups of rocks are sufficient, arranged with a large central piece and a couple of smaller ones placed close by. Then, using a coarse white quartz sand or fine gravel, which can also be obtained from large garden centers, cover all of the exposed areas of the ground to a depth of about two inches. This then needs to be raked carefully to produce the characteristic lines, with small wave-like circles arranged around the groups of rocks. You should also have a wooden veranda or patio facing the length of the garden, from which you may view the abstract scene of harmony that you have created.

ZEN AND THE ARTS

The Zen ideal is to be natural, spontaneous, and at one with all of creation. A whole lifetime might be spent in meditation, punctuated with brief flashes of illumination which imbue the student with an intense creative power expressing this ideal. Working with simple materials lying close at hand, such as a writing brush and paper, or the plants and trees growing in the mountains near the monastery, Zen followers were able to develop unique forms of artistic expression.

Reflecting its spiritual ideal, Zen Buddhism has expressed a profound simplicity, coupled with a poignant appreciation of the transience of life, seen nowhere else in the world. The art forms thus developed found their greatest flowering in Japan, where they resonated with pre-existing aesthetic trends. A true appreciation of Zen art enables us to look afresh at the world around us, while plumbing the depths of our spiritual being.

AND WHAT IS IT, THE HEART?
IT IS THE SOUND OF THE PINE BREEZE
IN THE BLACK INK PAINTING.
IKKYU (1394–1481 CE)

THE PLACE OF ZEN ART IN SOCIETY

As single-minded itinerant seekers of Enlightenment, the early Zen monks in China would have had little interest in, or involvement with, the arts. Even after a few generations when they began to settle down in monasteries, the rigors of work, supporting themselves, and the long hours of meditation would have made it unlikely that they would have had the time or inclination to develop specifically Zen styles of artistic expression. This had to wait many centuries, until Zen had become far more widely accepted—in China during the Song period. Nevertheless, there were not many areas of creative endeavor in China that can truly be said to be Zen in origin, perhaps because China is such a vast country with so many other competing fashions and styles. While some forms of expression had their origins in China, the true flowering of Zen art seems only to have taken place in Japan during the medieval period. Even there, such art forms were mainly the domain of the elite and had little connection with the culture of the common people.

The true flowering of Zen art did not take place in Japan until the medieval period.

In Japan also, much of what is now popularly thought to be Zen in origin was probably only refined by Zen masters, for there seems to have been a happy symbiosis between the pre-existent tastes of refined Japanese people and the predilections of Zen teachers. The history of art in Japan reveals something rather curious: there seem to be two parallel but unrelated trends in all forms of cultural or artistic expression. That is to say, there is a distinct liking for the novel, the gaudy, and the exotic, while at the same time, a strong inclination toward the understated and austere. It is almost as if the islands of Japan were occupied by two separate races of people who carried on their different traditions in society. This may not be as far-fetched as it sounds, considering the origins of Japanese society. Though it would be outside the scope of this book to go into great detail, it must be remembered that Japan was occupied for thousands of years by a group of people known by their characteristic cord-marked pottery—the Jomon. In recent years, archeological discoveries have begun to show that these people were far more sophisticated and culturally advanced than had been thought hitherto. Around 300 BCE, a wave of racially different people— known as the Yayoi—entered Japan from the mainland and established themselves as the dominant force in the land. The modern Japanese population is a mixture of these two races, as can be shown by genetic studies. In the early medieval period, this process of racial mixing was probably far less advanced and so may have given rise to different aesthetic tastes. Whatever the case, the cultural leaders in Japan often seemed to veer from one extreme to another in the type of artistic expression they favored.

The Japanese have made pots in two very distinct styles: novel, gaudy, and exotic on the one hand; understated and austere on the other.

JAPANESE AESTHETICS

Appreciation of the beauty of nature also contains a poignant awareness of the transience of all things.

For much of Japanese history, it was the court with its aristocrats, or the later ruling warrior class, who seem to have defined the codes of artistic taste. From the various writings that have survived from the Heian period (794–1185 CE) onward, we can detect a range of terminology that was used to describe the ideals of aesthetic experience, ever moving in the direction of the subtle and subdued. Indeed, for the nobility of the Heian period, appreciation of beauty was almost a way of life. Since most of these were adopted as criteria of Zen art forms, it will be useful to look at these now to gain an overview of the guiding principles that were adopted by Zen artists. First, it is probably true to say that the Japanese have always valued feeling over the intellect, and so we see that such terms that are used exclusively relate to emotional reactions to works of art in all areas.

The Heian aristocracy and intelligentsia considered that a true appreciation of the beautiful was possible only for those with exquisitely refined taste. The extremely delicate shades of color used to dye their silk robes, the muted delicacy of flowers, the sight of the reflected rays of the sun shining red through clouds—all of these things were said to be *miyabi* or "elegantly graceful." When encountering some unexpected beautiful sight, such as a cherry tree in full blossom or a splendid sunset, the nobility would cry out "*appare*" in their delight. A related word, *awaré*, was soon used to describe this "ah-ness" of things. It conveys that unexpected rise of emotion when contemplating a thing of beauty, coupled with a tinge of poignancy derived from the knowledge that it is ephemeral and will soon fade. This term continued to be used through the ages in Japan, and was later adopted and refined still further by Zen monks, with their heightened sense of impermanence derived from Buddhist teachings.

As the late Heian age moved into a dark period of uncertainty that was marked by widespread plagues, war, and destruction, their earlier love of the brash new imports from China and the gaudy display of wealth became muted. As though looking back to some lost age, people began to appreciate the calm beauty of old things. A sense of melancholy pervaded noble society, finding expression in the new aesthetic concept of *sabi*. The word *sabi* basically means "patina," the weathered look an object has when it has become mellowed by age. No longer did the new appeal to people living in the decaying splendor of the capital, but they came to treasure the tranquil air of old, weathered, and worn objects with their hint of melancholy and loneliness. This ideal too was to become firmly rooted in the minds of the artistic leaders of future generations, for it reflected their experience of the world.

Implicit in the idea, or rather the feeling, of *sabi* was the desire to avoid the showy and ornate. Instead, a studied restraint in all forms of artistic activity came to be seen as desirable. The Japanese termed this feeling *shibui*, a "sober astringency." This implied the discarding of all that was unnecessary, while valuing things which projected a subtle inner strength that is reserved and unassertive.

Finally, one further aesthetic concept, known as *yugen*, was developed at that time. *Yugen* is basically an extension of the complex sense of poignancy of *aware*. It is applied to things which are veiled and merely suggestive of some deep profundity. It later refers to an evocation of emotions that, through their depth and power, transcend verbal expression. While *aware* might refer to the beauty of a late summer sunset, *yugen* is like the encroaching darkness that spreads when the sun has almost set out of sight. This evocative sense of the profound was especially prized by later Zen masters—in their paintings, for example, when the viewer himself had to complete a picture that had merely been hinted at or suggested.

A female dancer of the Heian period, wearing the elaborate costume of a male courtier.

139

CALLIGRAPHY

Calligraphy was the most highly treasured art form in ancient China. To be sure, beautiful writing was appreciated in many other cultures, but it was still usually only a means to an end. Perhaps the only script that comes close to approaching Chinese in its innate beauty is Egyptian hieroglyphic writing, but the smaller range of hieroglyphs and the method of writing them meant they could never develop into anything resembling Chinese calligraphy. Most Chinese characters are not pictographs in the true sense. A character combines sound with meaning, while the shape itself often suggests that meaning.

The earliest examples of Chinese writing date back to rough symbols scratched on pieces of bone during the Shang period over four thousand years ago. It seems that soon afterward Chinese scribes began using brushes to write with, and they have done so ever since. Even though pens must have been known to them from their neighbors, who were influenced by Indian culture, and there are some rare examples from border outposts of Chinese characters written with a pen, the Chinese seem to have preferred the flexibility that the brush offers. A wide range of calligraphic styles is possible using a brush, from bold formal script to gossamer-like tracings that seem to dance upon the paper.

Calligraphy needs only four items: a brush, a stick of black ink, an ink-stone to grind the ink in water, and some paper, or possibly silk. The preparation for writing resembles a meditation in itself, requiring deep concentration, for it should be remembered that the absorbent nature of Chinese paper does not allow for any correction of mistakes. The calligrapher sits calmly, grinding the ink on the stone—a process that may take more than ten minutes. While doing this, he will often focus his attention on the theme or content of what he is about to write. When the moment comes to begin, the brush is lowered to the paper, and the writing flows forth with a careful balance of control and spontaneity. The brush allows great freedom, so watching a master calligrapher engaged in writing is akin to watching a dance that moves across the paper with grace and effortless skill.

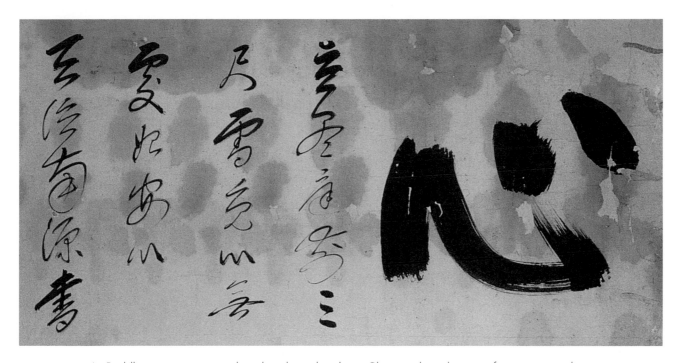

As Buddhist texts were introduced and translated into Chinese, the sole way of propagating these teachings was through handwritten copies. Indeed, even after printing was applied to the mass production of the Buddhist scriptures in the Northern Song period, handwritten copying of texts remained important and convenient for many centuries afterward in China and neighboring countries that used Chinese script, such as Japan and Korea. It was this association of calligraphy with learning, and the copying of scriptures, that led to Zen forms of calligraphy. As a way of expressing their mastery of teachings, Zen masters were attracted to the combination of controlled concentration with the spontaneity they valued so highly. Often their calligraphy is wild and almost abstract, an outpouring of powerful and sensuous meaning. Again, the natural contrast between the intense black of the ink and the white of the paper acted as an expression of Zen ideas. The blank whiteness of the paper suggests the untrammeled emptiness of reality that is all-pervading, with the black of tangible ephemeral forms erupting within that space, expressing a unity of the absolute with the relative.

This example of calligraphy by a Zen priest embodies the balance of control and concentration with spontaneity and flow that is so important to Zen thought.

SUMI-É

The black ink paintings known in Japanese as *sumi-é* are a natural and logical extension of calligraphy, for this style of painting uses exactly the same equipment. The origins of *sumi-é* probably lie with moments of relaxation which scribes managed to snatch during their work, doing small thumbnail caricatures and scenes, just as writers have always done. To be sure, there was a strong tradition in China of monochromatic painting that existed long before black ink paintings became popular, and eventually emerged as the favored manner of painting. Yet the use of monochrome, through the graded use of black ink, became extremely popular for a time during the late Tang and Song dynasties. Only the most experienced calligraphers—people endowed with sufficient artistic skill—were able to produce fine ink paintings. Just as with calligraphy, it took years of training to achieve the prized controlled spontaneity that is characteristic of this genre.

The mountains of China, with their grandeur and austere beauty, were a dominant feature represented in Zen landscape painting.

The artists working in this medium discovered that it was possible to create the illusion of color through the use of graded washes of black ink. As with the Japanese concept of *yugen*, the viewer transforms the subtle range of blacks and grays into a full-color scene in their mind. In other words, the picture is, in a sense, unfinished, and must be mentally completed by the viewer.

Since they used brush and ink for calligraphy, Zen masters were soon attracted to the possibilities offered by black ink painting. Several types of paintings were produced by these Zen monk painters. Initially, they confined themselves to small paintings to illustrate notable episodes in Zen legend, such as famous encounters between masters, often with a touch of the zany humor that is typical of Zen. Apart from these paintings, many fine portraits of Zen masters, both living and dead, were produced. The artists attempted to capture more than just the likeness of the master; they also tried to reveal the essence of that master's inner realization and Enlightenment. The many portraits of Bodhidharma are good examples of this.

It was only a little later that Zen artists turned themselves to the monochrome style of landscape painting which had developed in the wider artistic society of the time. These landscape paintings are not usually actual scenes, but idealized representations combining desired features from various sources. The later Japanese landscape painters painted Chinese scenes without even going to China! Each scene includes a range of fixed motifs, such as the ubiquitous mountains

A black ink portrait of the Bodhidharma. Zen painter monks produced many examples of this type of painting.

143

and crags, gnarled trees, rocks, some wildlife, and small hints of human habitation. Formally speaking, the scene is arranged in three layers, with the foreground shown in detail, the mid-distance in somewhat less detail, and finally the hazy mountains in the distance. Each band of representation is separated by billowing mist and cloud. Put together, the images suggest vast, numinous, empty spaces—rather like the stone gardens that such paintings inspired. For the Zen artists, those craggy mountains and gnarled, twisted trees were a way of representing the struggle that they and others had undergone to attain awakening.

There were several schools of black ink painting in the Song period, such as the Northern School with its sharp-edged angular brush strokes and formal symmetrical layout, the Southern School with its romantic, misty feel that uses soft ink washes and diffuse lighting. These two schools later merged to produce a composite style, through the efforts of Ma Yuan with his use of space,

sharp foregrounds, and soft distances, and Xia Gui who delighted in lines and silhouettes with trees and rocks in the foreground. But the heyday of black ink painting in China soon ended and by the Ming period it had completely gone out of fashion. It was through the Japanese Zen artists, who were enamored of this style, that such paintings continued and were refined.

The explicit connection between Zen and *sumi-é* was made in Japan under the patronage of the ruling elite during the Ashikaga period. The greatest Japanese artist in this field was Sesshu (1420–1507 CE). He traveled to China in the hope of improving his technique, but on his return he said that he had found little there to learn except from the landscape itself. Yet, in truth, his style does owe much to the late Ma-Xia school of ink painting for it combines an angularity of brush strokes with subtle tonal washes, just as in China. Curiously, his successors include such artists as Kano Masanobu, who developed the colorfully rich, decorative style of the Kano School in Kyoto.

Zen artists used landscapes to convey a sense of vast space and emptiness; this gnarled tree suggests the struggle for Enlightenment.

LITERATURE

As a way of life, Zen loves to embrace paradoxes. This is shown by the relationship between Zen and literature of all kinds. With the advent of Hui-neng, Zen became very anti-intellectual and iconoclastic. Its followers were urged to stop studying, to burn the scriptures and focus all of their attention on meditation alone. Yet, despite this attitude, the students of the great Zen masters busied themselves, from the start, compiling records of their masters' sayings, deeds, and sermons. These compilations became just as canonical for Zen followers as the orthodox scriptures of Buddhism that they had tried so hard to discard!

Yet, in at least one important aspect, they did differ from the orthodox scriptures, because they were written in a colloquial style of Chinese. In the early centuries of the Buddhist transmission to China, the translators incorporated many colloquial idioms in their work so that the Buddhist teachings would be understood by the ordinary person. But, as Buddhism became patronized by the emperor, and all new translations had to be submitted to him for approval, the style became increasingly formalized, and followed the idealized models of classical Chinese literature. This tended to make the import of the texts less obvious to those whose education fell short of the high scholarly standards of the day. In contrast, medieval Zen records in China use the language of the streets—rough and racy, sometimes bordering on the crude. Hui-neng's *Platform Sutra* is full of the Chinese equivalent of spelling mistakes and bad grammar, but therein lies its appeal.

With their interest in calligraphy, the Zen masters had to find something appropriate to express when they put brush to paper. As calligraphy is normally done on medium-sized, oblong pieces of paper that can later be mounted as a scroll, short poetic compositions were the most suitable for the Zen masters. One uniquely Zen type of composition is the famous death poem, known as *gata*, that forms the final testament of the master's teachings for his students. These were normally written shortly before death and encapsulate all that the master has accomplished. The *gata* written by the Japanese Zen master Ryokan (1758?–1831 CE) is an excellent example of the genre:

What shall be my legacy?
The blossoms of the spring,
The cuckoo in the hills,
The leaves of the autumn.

This expresses the Zen ideal of naturalness well—and the importance of letting things just be in a spirit of spontaneity, where the individual becomes at one with the world.

In Japan, the pinnacle of Zen poetry can be seen in the short telegram-like *haiku* poems. These miniature works, written in just three lines with a mere seventeen syllables, are quite unlike anything written anywhere else in the world. In their economy of words, they capture all the Zen ideals of poignant transience and delicate suggestiveness, leaving the audience to complete the picture for itself. In many cases, they are just a carefully chosen juxtaposition of brief phrases that somehow seem to convey far more than their individual parts would suggest. Take, for example, Basho's (1644–1694 CE) famous *haiku*:

An ancient pond
A frog jumps in
The sound of water

No translation can do justice to this *haiku*, hence the many versions that can be seen in English, each trying to grasp the spirit of the Japanese original. It is said that this was the *haiku*

The Japanese haiku *may capture a fleeing moment within the world of nature.*

composed by Basho at the moment of his initial Zen awakening. In his youth, he was a samurai, but, on the death of his master, he was homeless and became a monk. He diligently studied all the venerated scriptures of Zen Buddhism and could quote convincingly as the occasion demanded. Yet one day a Zen master patiently chided him for his lack of originality. The master challenged

Basho to say something of his own understanding of Buddhism without relying on the words of others. Lost for words, he is said to have sat in silence for some time until he heard the sound of a frog jumping into a pond nearby. The poem burst forth from his lips at that moment, and he experienced a flash of awakening.

I would like to close this section with one of my favorite *haiku* poems, written by a little-known poet in the nineteenth century:

The winter seagull—

In life, no home

In death, no grave

NOH THEATER

Like many other art forms in Japan, the theater also has its roots in Chinese imports during the Heian period and before. Early theater in Japan took the form of *sarugaku*, farcical dance stories with a strong touch of earthy indecency. These were often performed as counterbalancing parodies of the solemn ritual dances of the Shinto shrines. Actors in such dance dramas are known to have used masks, with their performances accompanied by drums and flutes. In time these dramas gradually evolved into something akin to Western medieval morality plays—entertaining, sometimes moving, but not great art. In fact, they still survive as the *kyogen* or comic interludes that are still performed alongside *noh* plays.

The precise origin of *noh* theater is uncertain, but a key development can be pinpointed with accuracy. A fourteenth-century actor named Kannami, who seems to have performed some prototype *noh* plays, had a son named Zeami who was also an actor. They were performing before Ashikaga Yoshimitsu, who was to become a great patron of the arts and Zen. Yoshimitsu was attracted to Zeami and took him as a lover—homosexuality was common and accepted in Japan at that time. With the support of Yoshimitsu, Zeami was to become the father of *noh* drama, and the author of much of its repertoire. Zeami defined the basic characteristics, techniques, and performance styles of *noh* drama to such an extent that soon after his death *noh* became a static art form which, even today, is still performed as it was some six hundred years ago.

The *noh* stage is a bare platform of polished wood about twenty feet square. It is raised above the ground a few feet, and projects out into audience like a shrine, under a heavy roof supported by pillars. A covered ramp leads from the right of the stage to wings, with three small pine trees set on it. The backdrop to the stage itself

With the minimum of dialog and scenery, noh theater explores extreme emotions such as guilt, love, or jealousy.

depicts a large gnarled pine, just in front of which sit a small number of musicians. The ground encircling the stage itself is covered by a band of sand, with a small set of steps at front of stage. The *noh* stage is often in the semi-open air, rather like the Elizabethan theaters that it somewhat resembles. The performances have no other scenery than the pine trees, and few props are used. The performance is accompanied by a flautist who plays the characteristic *noh* flute, with its unique high, piercing sound, and also by two drummers who play the unusual hourglass-shaped drums—one large, one small. The rhythm of the performance is punctuated by eerie interjections and cries from the drummers. Apart from these musicians, who sit at the back of the stage, there is a chorus of about eight men wearing formal, dark kimonos on the left of the stage.

A *noh* drama is a strange experience for a Westerner, for it is quite different from anything traditionally performed in the West. It combines haunting poetry with a subdued intensity of acting and mournful music. The main actor is almost always masked as he delivers his performance. The lacquered wooden *noh* masks are highly treasured artifacts, often hundreds of years old, that are capable of suggesting various expressions as they are moved and inclined in the light. The whole performance proceeds slowly with chanted poetry and slow-motion dance. *Noh* plays rarely tell a story as we would expect, but instead focus on some tragic event. They are a medium used for exploring extreme emotions of love, hatred, guilt, or jealousy.

The restraint with which the intensity of the emotion is suggested—with the minimum of dialog and scenery—exemplifies the aesthetic ideal of *yugen*, and thus was particularly pleasing to the supporters and practitioners of Zen in medieval Japan. Most of the other Japanese artistic ideals can also be seen in a *noh* setting—*sabi* in the age of the old masks and costumes, the gray timbers of the stage itself, *shubui* in the restrained acting and movements, and *awaré* in the intensely poignant music with its undertones of unspeakable loneliness and sadness. Because it combines many of the ideals so favored by Zen esthetes, one might almost say that *noh* is the Zen art form *par excellence* in Japan—if it were not for the tea ceremony, which must take that place.

The wooden masks used in noh drama are treasured artifacts, and are designed to suggest a range of different emotions.

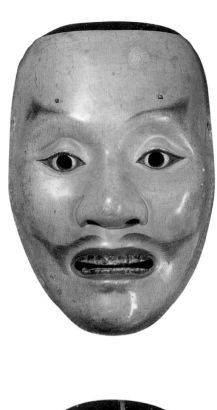

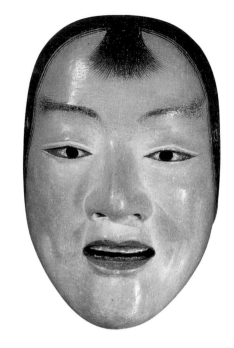

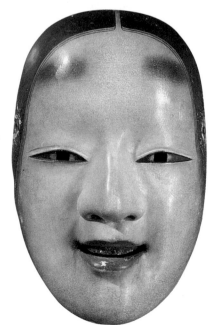

THE TEA CEREMONY

The history of tea in China is lost in the mists of history. In the earliest times, it was probably only drunk medicinally, and, even in the Tang period, it was hardly drunk at all. At that time, tea leaves were smoked and squashed together in the form of bricks. When it was drunk, it was boiled with salt, and sometimes other ingredients were added, such as ginger. It was only later, in the Song period, that tea drinking was to become more popular. Instead of the strong, earthy flavor of smoked brick tea, green leaves were ground and whisked together with hot water. Though not originally connected with Zen, tea was a little-known drink until the Song period, though it had probably been drunk by Buddhist monks because of the caffeine content that helped to keep them awake during long meditation sessions. Indeed, there is a charming legend linking tea with Bodhidharma. During the years he spent meditating in front of a wall, he is said to have dozed off on one occasion. Out of frustration, he took a razor and sliced off his eyelids so that he would

The tea ceremony in Japan is highly ritualized, involving the use of several traditional utensils.

no longer be able to shut them in sleep. A tea shrub is said to have magically sprouted up where they fell on the ground!

Inevitably, a form of tea drinking was introduced into Japan in the eighth century from China, but it remained an aristocratic drink at court—nothing more than an expensive import which was drunk, but probably not enjoyed, as a status symbol. Some tea is supposed to have been grown in Japan at this time and afterward, but it only gained popularity much later. The Zen monk Eisai, who visited China during the thirteenth century, reintroduced and popularized the habit, which had become fashionable in China at the time.

The roots of the Japanese tea ceremony are linked to Zen monasteries in China, where monks would hold a commemorative ceremony of tea drinking in front of a portrait of Bodhidharma, passing around a single bowl of tea, which they shared. No doubt Eisai would have been familiar with this practice, and introduced this ritualized manner of tea drinking to Japan. Like so many other Zen art forms, the tea ceremony became popular through the patronage of the Ashikaga nobility. The great patron of Zen culture, Ashikaga Yoshimasa, had a simple tearoom constructed in one of his residences along monastic lines, which featured many of the things we now associate with the tea ceremony, such as the *tokonoma*, a flower arrangement, and, above all, the sharing of a single cup.

In present-day Japan, the tea ceremony ritual still flourishes.

However, though influenced by Zen masters, the earlier tea ceremony in Japan was still a fairly lavish ritual reflecting the ornate style of its Song original. Yet, as time went by, a reaction set in against this excessive luxury. Soon, tea ceremony aficionados had small thatched tea huts built for themselves, set in private gardens. Instead of the expensive Song celadon, rugged folk pottery produced in Japan was favored, since it suggested the Zen ideal of refined poverty. The acme of the tea ceremony was reached with the great tea-master Sen no Rikyu (1521–1591 CE). He was tea instructor to both Oda Nobunaga and Toyotomi

With its sparse setting and intense focus and concentration, the tea ceremony shares many elements with Zen meditation.

Hideyoshi, the two great warlords who began the process of reunifying Japan after decades of civil war. The modern form of the tea ceremony derives from his alterations to the earlier more elaborate style. It was Sen no Rikyu who introduced one further aesthetic concept to the Japanese—*wabi. Wabi* implies the sense of restraint and "artificial" poverty that appealed to the refined connoisseurs of the tea ceremony who were strongly influenced by Zen philosophy.

As standardized by Rikyu, the tea ceremony uses few utensils in a small, plain room adorned with only a single flower in a vase in the *tokonoma*, perhaps with a choice piece of calligraphy hanging from the wall behind. The utensils themselves are chosen for their conformity to the most refined ideals of simplicity and restraint. They include little more than a lacquered tea container, a kettle on a charcoal hearth recessed into the floor, a bamboo dipper, a bamboo whisk that resembles a shaving brush, and a single tea bowl of simple pottery. After due preparations have been made, the green tea powder is placed in the bowl and whisked with silent, thoughtful ritual. It is then passed to the guest of honor, who takes a few sips and passes it on to the next person. When the tea has been drunk, a second cup is prepared and drunk in the same way. Afterward, the guests relax a little and admire the treasured utensils or the beauty of the flower arrangement. With intense concentration focused on the sparse interior of the tearoom, the tea ceremony greatly resembles a Zen meditation session and, for this reason, was highly favored by Zen masters.

The utensils chosen for the tea ceremony embody the Zen ideals of restraint and simplicity.

CERAMICS

Closely related to the tea ceremony is the appreciation of certain forms of pottery that evolved at the time of Sen no Rikyu. Pottery has a long history in Japan—the oldest known pieces in the world, dating from 10,000 BCE, have been found there. With this centuries-long tradition, it is surprising that the Japanese relied heavily on mainland inspiration for centuries after the first cultural contacts were forged with China. Korean stoneware and Tang color-glazed pottery were imported and copied for some time, but were not really in harmony with the earthy native spirit of the Japanese people and their taste for simple, natural forms. To be sure, the beautiful celadon pottery of the Song period, with its delicate, blue-green, translucent glazes, was widely used in tea ceremonies at first, but even this was felt by Rikyu to be out of place in his austere Zen style of tea ceremony.

Raku pottery, with its controlled "imperfections," perfectly captures the spirit of Zen and is ideal for the tea ceremony.

One day, it is said, he found a roughly glazed tile and saw in it the ideal form for which he had been looking. He employed Chojiro, a Korean potter living in Kyoto, to create the new approved pattern of tea bowls. This style became known as *raku*, meaning "comfortable" or "pleasurable." *Raku* bowls are not coiled or thrown, but rather the clay is shaped and molded by hand like sculpture. Instead of the normal controlled, gradual firing of high quality Chinese-style pottery, the bowls are thrust straight into red-hot kilns as tiles are, to give them the desired rough *sabi* appearance, with all its interesting cracks and imperfections. The glaze, often black, but sometimes red or off-white, bubbles and runs freely on the surface of the bowl, which is devoid of all other decoration. It is the imperfections that occur spontaneously through "controlled" accidents that give *raku*-ware its unique characteristics—which Rikyu believed captured the true spirit of the Zen tea ceremony.

IKEBANA

As well as creating a new aesthetic standard in tea ceremony ceramics, Rikyu was also responsible for the Zen style of flower arrangement (*ikebana*). In many ways, the artistic display of flowers is appropriate in Zen Buddhism, given the legendary origins of Zen itself, which tell of the Buddha transmitting the quintessence of his teachings to Kashyapa when he held up a flower in silence on the Vulture's Peak. Apart from this, flowers had always formed part of the basic set of sacred offerings placed on shrines in Buddhism, together with lamps and incense.

The Japanese connection with formal flower arrangements dates back to the early days of Buddhism in that country. A certain Ono no Imoko visited China several times as an ambassador in the seventh century, and, after his retirement, he was appointed as the guardian and abbot of the Rokkaku-do temple in Kyoto. The small house adjacent to the temple where he took up his residence was known as *ike-no-bo* ("the hut by the pond"). There he devoted his time to developing the devotional arrangement of flowers he had learned in China. It is from this that the oldest surviving school of flower arrangement developed, retaining the name *ike-no-bo*, which was associated with Ono no Imoko.

The early style of flower arrangement was mainly practiced for display in the large halls of temples and aristocratic mansions. It was known as *rikka* or "standing flowers" and was characterized by large, exuberant structures, some of which are said to have been over fifteen feet tall. The *rikka* style employed complex symbolism regarding the size and positioning of the component flowers and branches, for they were intended to be stylized representations of the universe offered to the buddhas. By the fifteenth century, a number of manuals on the art of flower arrangement had been written, and so the art gradually became both popular and secularized, especially through the patronage of Ashikaga Yoshimasa (1435–1490 CE). By this time, certain Zen

preferences had begun to make themselves felt, with much striving for natural appearance and more asymmetrical layouts. The Japanese name for flower arrangement is *ikebana*, which conveys the idea of setting out flowers in a natural way that brings the display to life. Like the Zen landscape gardens, the flower arrangements were created through a carefully contrived naturalness. Indeed, these flower arrangements could be considered to be the indoor equivalents of gardens, so people living in apartments can also have miniature gardens.

As with landscape gardens, the Japanese art of flower arranging aims at a carefully created air of naturalness.

As with a number of other art forms at the time, the tea master Sen no Rikyu totally transformed the elaborate *rikka* style, which he considered to be too lavish and lacking in the simplicity of *wabi* for the purposes of his tea ceremonies. So he developed the austere *nageire* style of arrangement, which relied on just one or two choices of stems in a vase. This display was placed in the *tokonoma* for the delight of guests at tea ceremonies. In the eyes of the Zen tea masters, the flowers symbolized the human connection with nature, and were a unifying bridge between the human and natural worlds.

As Japan settled into a long era of peace from the seventeenth century onward, a new bourgeois class emerged which adopted many of the Zen art forms with suitable modifications. For these people, the *rikka* style was too grandiose, while the *nageire* style was too austere. A compromise was developed which combined elements from both styles, and the current form of *ikebana* known as *seika* came into being. Moreover, the art of flower arrangement had been exclusively a male preserve, but the changing role of women in conjunction with the smaller size of the arrangements led to greater participation by women in *ikebana*.

A Zen flower arrangement
should convey a sense of
restraint and harmony, bringing
the natural world into the home.

PRACTICAL ZEN: *IKEBANA*

Several distinct schools of flower arrangement are popular in Japan today. It is obviously impossible to explain the technique for arranging flowers in detail here, as people study its subtleties for decades. But it is important to remember the underlying aesthetics of simplicity, naturalness, and suggestion. The arrangement produced by a master is a careful understatement of controlled artifice that seems totally natural and brings out the best from the flowers. The Japanese pay much attention to the seasonality of the flowers used, so try to obtain ones that are in season. You should also avoid gaudy blossoms that are not natural to the country where you are living. The vase should ideally be restrained in design, possibly a handmade ceramic container, which can be either flat or jar-shaped. The overall color should not clash or deflect attention from the flowers, but work in harmony with them. You will need a special item known as a *kenzan* for placing the flowers in position. This object has a series of small nails or pins that are set into a heavy lead base; it is now easily obtained from many suppliers in the West.

When arranging flowers, always strive for balance and harmony; remember, less is better than more for the Zen feel. Traditionally, there is a definite structure to the arrangement; a larger central stem is placed in the middle, while several short ones are judiciously placed around it. Be sure to use a reasonable amount of greenery in the arrangement, although excess leaves should be stripped from flower stems. When completed, water should be put into the vase. Then the finished arrangement should be placed somewhere uncluttered, where it will serve as an inspirational reminder of the natural world outside.

INDEX